BET
ON
BLACK

BET
ON
BLACK

THE GOOD NEWS ABOUT BEING BLACK IN AMERICA TODAY

EBONI K. WILLIAMS

LEGACY
LIT

NEW YORK BOSTON

Legacy Lit
Hachette Book Group
1290 Avenue of the Americas
New York, NY 10104
LegacyLitBooks.com
Twitter.com/LegacyLitBooks
Instagram.com/LegacyLitBooks

First Edition: January 2023

Legacy Lit is an imprint of Grand Central Publishing. The Legacy Lit name and logo are trademarks of Hachette Book Group, Inc.

The publisher is not responsible for websites (or their content) that are not owned by the publisher.

The Hachette Speakers Bureau provides a wide range of authors for speaking events. To find out more, go to hachettespeakersbureau.com or email HachetteSpeakers@hbgusa.com.

Legacy Lit books may be purchased in bulk for business, educational, or promotional use. For information, please contact your local bookseller or the Hachette Book Group Special Markets Department at special.markets@hbgusa.com.

Library of Congress Control Number: 2022947909

ISBNs: 9780306828645 (hardcover), 9780306828669 (ebook)

Printed in Canada

MRQ-T

10 9 8 7 6 5 4 3 2 1

I dedicate this book to Carey James Williams, Sr., and Gloria J. Williams. My grandfather and mother were the first two people to show me the power of what happens when you Bet on Black.

I also dedicate this book to the Black people in America. We have always bet on ourselves . . . and we always will.

CONTENTS

BET
ON
BLACK

OPENING STATEMENT

"I find, in being black, a thing of beauty, a joy, a strength, a secret cup of gladness."

—Ossie Davis

I AM IN A DEEP LOVE AFFAIR with my Blackness.

I carry my Blackness with me everywhere I go, boldly, proudly, audaciously...*unapologetically.* Whether I'm on *The Real Housewives of New York*, on *The View*, or on my podcast *Holding Court*, I'm Blackity-Black Black, pro-Black, perennially centering Blackness, whatever you want to call it. I can talk about Blackness through any angle or lens, whether as a court-appointed legal adviser or on the couch with my girls in some chic Walker Wear sweats talking shit. I can talk about being Black *all* day, *every* day, *however* way. I carry my Blackness with me into every room I enter, whether serving as a public defender, private defense lawyer, television journalist, executive producer, event host, or reality TV show cast member. My mode of Blackness has been informed by Southern sensibilities, academic achievement, and the oft-intense glare of media. My Blackness has nurtured my spirit, and I wrote *Bet on Black* to feed yours as well.

We've long been aware that Blackness has been perceived by some as a threat, as an unacceptable breach of an American social contract that, for centuries, has proclaimed brown skin to be an inferior marker of identity. As seen with slavery and Jim Crow laws, this dehumanizing contract proclaims that our heritage should be downplayed and subcategorized, permanently positioned as an afterthought in the collective consciousness. Some might argue that we've moved past these notions of inferiority and become an egalitarian society, but as Black people we know that's ridiculously naive and dishonest. We know that a racist social contract still exists in the minds of many and continues to shape our society's institutions. Regardless of these realities, I wrote this book to unite us so that we can collectively refuse to have our futures dictated by anti-Black nonsense.

Since the early seventeenth century, when Africans were first brought to American colonial shores, ideas of Blackness have been associated with a subordinate, undesirable experience codified in law for centuries. This is a lie maintained by a white power structure invested in maintaining supremacy at all costs. We now know how utterly arbitrary and mind-numbing this bottom-tier human assignment always was. There have been countless books celebrating the traditional American social order, which requires the dominance of whiteness, heterosexuality, Christianity, and maleness. Whiteness is inherently inflated in this rather tired mix, and if we start to do the work of telling the truth about ourselves as Black people, then we can build an environment for ourselves where we can truly live and thrive. We don't need to depend on anyone else to give us freedom. We never have. We can ensure our full liberation by starting with a basic truth—that everything we've been taught, told, and force-fed about white positioning in this nation and beyond is completely arbitrary.

Yes, it's made up. And once certain folks have stopped clutching their pearls at this assertion, we can go about the great work of figuring out what this means for Blackness. Whiteness has been inflated, placed high on a pedestal, and positioned as superior, which means that what we've been told all of our lives about the positioning of Blackness as inferior and subordinate is just as arbitrary.

It's why, as we cellularly move through life and handle our day-to-day, we should no longer buy into subordinate positions based on our skin color. It's a very American notion to say that Black people have a place in every space they occupy and that this space is always secondary to that of whiteness. We need to be extremely hostile to that assignment. This subordinate ranking is as false and made up as the tooth fairy, and we have to start treating it as such for the sake of our individual freedoms and collective well-being.

The good news about being Black today is that we can place our history, self-awareness, and understanding of who we are in this world front and center. We can let others contend with their comfort or discomfort with our choices as we refuse to succumb to projections of inferiority or second-class citizenship. These projections have nothing to do with who we are. Let's blow up the bullshit. Let's stop placating others or being silently complicit with racist lies and tell the truth: Blackness is and always has been deserving of a first-class, mainstream, fully liberated experience. Let's spread the good news about being Black in America with a fresh, unfettered celebration of self.

For years the prevailing narrative was that Blackness was something to manage, downplay, quiet, suppress, distract from, even erase. With *Bet on Black*, I'm flipping that paradigm on its head by maintaining that Blackness is a treasure to lead with. Blackness deserves to be centered. Black folks today need to bring their Blackness with them into every space they enter and occupy. Despite the racist fearmongers, a push to create space for Blackness isn't about mass white displacement. It's about allowing Black bodies and brains to occupy spaces with confidence, with an informed, well-thought-out process through which we readily wield power.

It's about recognizing that we have every right to access resources, professional opportunities, wealth, and the full emotional spectrum of the human condition in the same way that our white counterparts have done for eons.

I wrote this book because history shows it's common for Black folks to contend with manifestations of white insecurity that would have us become caricatures of who we really are or be removed from the playing field altogether. I want us to celebrate the expansiveness of our experiences, to honor this precious thing popularly known as Black excellence, to abjectly refuse subordinate positioning in everything that we do and in whatever way we define Blackness. *Bet on Black* is ultimately about reframing and reimagining our possibilities as a people. When we open and alter our own states of mind as they relate to racial identity, we embrace processes that will create a different reality for what it is to be Black in America.

I penned *Bet on Black* to help others in my community avoid the trap of white judgment and the limiting of our potential. I want Black folks to divorce ourselves from white comfort and white expectations and be concerned only with the preservation of our divine authentic selves. Whatever feels good to you is what you need to be in exclusive relationship with. And listen, I know a lot of us are out here trying to get chosen by somebody, so here's your opportunity... to choose your own damn self. Figure out how you want to carry your Blackness with you in whatever room you occupy, whether it's an office, a classroom, a café, a courtroom, or a TV show set. Let others reconcile their comfort with your choice...they're working through whatever they're working through, and it's not on you. Your job is to figure out who you are in this world while letting people simply deal with it.

Over the course of this book, I'll present key ideas that I believe are essential to embodying Blackness while sharing aspects of my personal experience that are relevant to whatever we're exploring. Think of what's to come as a meditation on interconnected concepts that I'm sure will produce a range of emotions. I'm going to flow and do my best to guide y'all along. I'll also provide occasional key takeaways—aka Bet on Black Moves—that I hope will inspire readers to walk an exceptional walk. Readers can expect shout-outs to specific historical events and contemporary figures who exemplify a Bet on Black consciousness, who've unabashedly occupied rooms and expectations with panache and flair. These public luminaries had the vision to pave a way for themselves with trailblazing work that exemplifies what we're capable of even when faced with oppression. And along the way, I'll give glimpses into my own life, providing anecdotes that I hope will be of service to readers and offering some insight into the trials and tribulations of your beloved Auntie E. I'm going to make myself vulnerable on the page because I believe that's the only way to grow, to share hon-estly and forthrightly and encourage others to do the same.

On top of all of this, I've provided a literary reference guide at the back of the book for readers who want to do more research on the topics I'll be exploring. But for those who just want to read *Bet on Black* and be done, never fear, I've got you. I've done the work so you don't have to.

I want *Bet on Black* to get people talking. You don't have to agree with me, as I'm aware that some of my opinions might feel controversial and against the grain. It's okay if you don't see eye to eye with me about everything. I just want you to think about the issues I raise, ask yourself questions, ask your friends and family questions, and start looking at how we see ourselves as Black folks in this nation with a fresh lens. If my words can help accomplish that, I'm happy.

I'm confident that the more we can recognize and embrace the power of our identities and history, prioritizing the authenticity of Blackness, the more readily we can create the paths that will allow us to walk contently in our joy and happiness.

So, are you ready for some good news?

CHAPTER 1

ACCURACY

"The South believed an educated Negro to be a dangerous Negro. And the South was not wholly wrong; for education among all kinds of men always has had, and always will have, an element of danger and revolution, of dissatisfaction and discontent."

—W. E. B. Du Bois,
The Souls of Black Folk

I'M THE COMPLETE AND TOTAL SHIT because the blood of Harriet Tubman runs through my veins.

The spirit of Tubman informs the lives of all Black people in America, of all our ancestors who survived soul-deadening subjugation. Her blood runs through the veins of all of us who stand on this land and dare to proclaim, "I'm here, so y'all need to make way."

When I walk into a space and people witness my audacity, when I insist on taking up space and saying what I think and feel and know, it's because I'm decidedly pushing against a narrative that tells me I'm less than. I'm refusing to accept a narrative that says I'm inferior, with a worthless, subordinate history. I'm not staying in an arbitrarily assigned "place" of lower or less. I know the truth, that my history—*our history*—is rich, layered, whether I choose to focus on the Black American experience or trace our roots back to Africa or explore the global diaspora. And this is a truth that I was fortunate to have known since childhood. Once I sit with the glorious expanse of my history, of our history, I have to pinch myself, because it's remarkable, even with the pain and tragedy, for it's also resilient, brilliant, and complex. And once again I have to say to myself with a smile, *I'm the complete and total shit.*

I'm making these statements to be provocative, yes, and to hopefully make you smile, but I'm also very serious about what I believe here: knowing our actual story is an essential part of having an advanced, fully liberated Black American experience. We've seen far too much evidence over the years of how we've internalized notions of inferiority that were created by a white supremacist society.

Perhaps the most famous symbol of this internalization is the doll test of the 1940s. For those of you who don't know, this was an experiment conducted by the wife-and-husband team of Mamie Phipps Clark and Kenneth Clark, two trailblazing Black intellectuals who were the first Black Americans to receive their PhDs from Columbia University, after having attended Howard University. In their study, a large group of Black children between the ages of three and seven in both Arkansas and Massachusetts were given the choice of four dolls to play with: two Black dolls with brown hair, two white dolls with blond hair. Most of the kids chose the white doll, seeing the white doll as having preferable characteristics. To make matters even worse, when the Black participants in the study were asked to identify with the Black dolls in some way—makes sense, right?—some of the kids lost it, breaking out into tears, not being comfortable with the association. To be clear, this means that Black children couldn't bear the thought of self-identifying with the toys that directly represented who they are.

We should all be outraged at this element of our history and the ideas of subordination that have been ingrained in us. The doll test was later used as a key component by the NAACP as they litigated the *Brown v. Board of Education* case that reached the Supreme Court. *Brown v. Board* ended the notion of "separate but equal" and declared school segregation illegal throughout the United States. The case relied on words from one of Dr. Kenneth Clark's papers based on the doll test: "To separate [Black American children] from others of similar age and qualifications solely because of their race generates a feeling of inferiority as to their status in the community that may affect their hearts and minds in a way unlikely ever to be undone."

Okay, so some of y'all may be wondering, *Why is Eboni bringing this up?* This is bullshit that went down more than seventy years ago and we've come a long way. After all we've accomplished with the civil rights, Black Power, and Black Lives Matter movements, with all of the TV shows and films and theatrical productions we've pushed to create and be a part of, surely Black people know their worth at this point, right?

Not necessarily.

From my own observations, I believe many of us would still pick the white doll with blond hair today. Sure enough, another brilliant sister, the scholar Toni Sturdivant, took the time to update the study. Soon after Sturdivant's daughter started to attend a predominantly white preschool, the little girl came home and said she didn't want to have brown skin, yearning to have blue eyes like her classmates. (Now for those of y'all in the know, this statement hearkens back of course to *The Bluest Eye*, the 1970 debut novel from future Nobel Prize–winning author Toni Morrison. In the book, she groundbreakingly deconstructed racism and self-hatred via an eleven-year-old Black girl with an all-consuming desire to look white.)

Inspired by her daughter's pain and her own personal horror, Sturdivant wanted to better understand how Black kids see their identity. She revisited the Clarks' doll test but addressed some of the methodologies of the original study. She was concerned that the Black kids in the Clarks' study were being interviewed in unnatural, potentially stressful conditions that could distort their responses. So she ended up observing Black girls for a year in a racially diverse pre-school setting with no direct interaction from an adult clinician. She later published her findings in the peer-reviewed academic journal *Early Childhood Education* in 2020.

The girls in her study had the option of playing with a darker-skinned Black doll, a lighter-skinned Black doll, a white doll, and a doll positioned as Latinx. Sturdivant observed that the Black girls routinely favored the Latinx and white dolls, choosing not to play with the Black dolls or do the Black dolls' hair. Sometimes the Black children in fact stepped on or over the Black dolls to get to other toys. Keep in mind they didn't treat the white and Latinx girls so disdainfully. And when they did choose the Black dolls, the girls tended to treat them in abusive ways, again differing from how they treated the lighter-skinned dolls. One girl even placed one of the Black dolls in a toy pot and pretended to cook it.

I mean, do I really need to say more? Are you outraged? Embarrassed? Undone? Wondering how the hell this could be our reality in the 2020s? After all the Black Girl Magic memes, Black Girls Rock telecasts, and My Black Is Beautiful hashtags, I've occasionally found myself legitimately shocked that we are still here. But I shouldn't be, and neither should you. Five to one. That's the ratio of how many positive comments are needed to cancel or outweigh a negative comment. Social science researchers Emily Heaphy and Marcial

Losada identified this five-to-one ratio, and it stands. So of course a relative handful of social media posts and newly created messages of Black girl awesomeness are not going to undo the hundreds of years of narrative around Black girls as ugly, undesirable, nappy headed, (sexually) fast, angry, and bad. I'll tell you why this madness is still happening with our kids, but also so often within ourselves as adults. It comes from a lack of centering Blackness in our history, from a lack of understanding where we come from, what we've survived, how fuckin' *dope* we are to have survived such bullshit, and what we're truly able to do when we seize opportunities.

Take a minute to think about the implications of Sturdivant's work: What do her observations mean for the future of the kids profiled in the study if this is how they treat self-representations? As they get older, will these girls continue to see Blackness as occupying a subordinate position in America? How will this affect their prospects in the world, their decisions around career and relationships? What type of work will they have to do later in life to overcome this distortion of their identity as inferior, as someone fit to be discarded? What will they have to do to see themselves as beautiful and grand, skilled and talented, deserving to be chosen for a variety of opportunities in their fine Black skin?

I think these questions point to why there were so many videos posted on social media of Black children losing their mind over the sight of Disney's trailer for the 2023 film *The Little Mermaid*. As most of y'all probably know by now, the title character is played by Black singer and performer Halle Bailey. I think our kids were shocked to see a Black Ariel because they just didn't think that occupying that sort of exalted role in a fantasy setting is supposed to be for them, based on generations of conditioning in America. A Black mermaid should be one of the most normal things we see in a mass entertainment context, greeted with a certain degree of excitement but also nonchalance. Why shouldn't we be spotlighted in this way? At disturbingly young ages, our kids have absorbed this idea that they're *still* supposed to occupy a lower caste in America. The messages are loud, consistent, and pervasive. Our media (and yes, that includes the news) tells us that Black girls "fight," that we are fast in the pants and no boy or man actually will want us unless we lower ourselves by resorting to desperate seduction, and we're told that our appearance will always be measured against, and inevitably fall short of, the universal holy grail of the global beauty standard: the white, Eurocentric, female aesthetic. We're all supposed to be blond, thin, white skinned, straight haired, and blue eyed—or damn close to it. And that's completely unacceptable.

I don't want to oversimplify things by stating that knowing our history is the only thing to consider when constructing a path toward Black self-empowerment and self-esteem.

And I know some of y'all might be rolling your eyes thinking about your more militant sisters and brothers who've been spouting the "know your history" talk for years. But they're absolutely right in their assertion that Black history is an essential component of positioning ourselves and future generations for success. An accurate and complete understanding of the Black experience, particularly our historical narrative, is inextricably linked to an actualized Black identity in today's America. And as someone who knows her history, I just don't trust that American schools are going to ever systematically do right by us. We have to do the work collectively on our own, for our kids but also for ourselves. We have to keep in mind that so much of our work as adults is about overcoming these notions of subordination that we internalized as kids, bestowed upon us by an anti-Black way of life.

I actually attribute much of my ability to *not* be subordinate later in life to being brought up in a household with Ms. Gloria and Ms. Katie, my mother and grandmother. They taught me that I should never perceive my skin color as being a deficiency. At the same time, I had access to books that centered our history...our truth.

All right, y'all, I'm going to move away from the subject of our collective history to spill some tea about my *own* personal history. Let me give a little snapshot of where and how I was raised: I grew up on the west side of Charlotte,

North Carolina, a historically Black working-class part of town, in the Ponderosa apartments complex, which consisted of rows of subsidized duplex homes. This was during the 1980s, a time of peak government project experiments when municipal funds were being allocated to lower-middle-class neighborhoods. Even though I didn't have a full understanding of what it meant to live in what would be called subsidized housing, I did have an awareness that there had to be a reason why all of Ponderosa looked the same. The reddish-brown sameness of the homes signaled something that I couldn't quite put my finger on. All I had to do was gaze across the street to look upon what I would one day understand to be private houses with manicured façades and beautiful floral gardens. These homes were occupied by members of the Black community who were educators, government employees, or factory workers. Ponderosa, though certainly clean and pristine in its own way, just wasn't pretty in the way the homes across the street were. In our gardens, you had green hedges, some grass... and, well, that was it. *And* we were supposed to be happy we had even that. We lived off of West Boulevard, and farther down this street were the actual projects, Boulevard Homes and Little Rock Homes. These were the rougher, stereotypical urban housing development towers you might think of from films like *New Jack City* or *Candyman* or the television show *Good Times*. At Ponderosa, we were squarely in the middle.

(Please don't get it twisted, though: I have no problem with a red-brick, sky-high, "project-looking" building. I lived in one for five years when I first moved to NYC…and this was *with* a six-figure salary. Yes, ma'am! No shame in my game. I lived in the Riverton in Harlem. While beautiful on the inside and attached to a $2,000-plus monthly fee for a one-bedroom unit, it definitely shouted "the projects" with its exterior. But hey, if it was good enough for James Baldwin, former NYC mayor David Dinkins, legendary jazz pianist Billy Taylor, and countless World War II veterans, then it was absolutely good enough for my Black ass. But back to the Ponderosa.)

Growing up, I lived in a two-bedroom apartment with my mother, Gloria, my grandmother, Katie, and at various times my two aunts, Sherry and Barbara. These four women were my pillars, having all participated in raising me in some way. My mother, born in 1960, was a highly ambitious woman who nonetheless was reared in the Jim Crow South. As a child she saw how structural racism killed dreams and stifled hope in her community. Her own mother, my grandmother, had spent much of her life centering the demands of white families, having worked as a domestic. My mother wanted something different for herself, regularly centering her ambition and drive over the desires of white people. And she certainly wanted something different for me.

This was why, when I started kindergarten at four years

old, she decided that I would be bused over from my neighborhood to Sharon Elementary. This school was located in southeast Charlotte, which is moneyed and predominantly white, and my mother knew that I could benefit from the district's wealth and resources. Being bused to a highly resourced educational institution set me up for opportunities that many of my other peers who attended schools in my town didn't have access to. At the same time, I began to experience a sense of otherness I'd never known.

I became one of the few Black girls in a classroom full of mostly white students, contending with racial realities whether I wanted to or not. Tears flooded my eyes one afternoon when I realized that I hadn't been invited to a classmate's birthday party, as the other girls had been, simply because of the color of my skin, a dynamic explained to me by my aunt Sherry. She was always crazy forthright with me when discussing race, believing that her niece needed to be prepared for the fucked-up ways of the world even as a kindergartner. Like my aunt, my mother also keenly understood all the horrific false narratives associated with Blackness. She made it her job—on top of the several other jobs she worked—to counter these narratives at every turn, creating strategies that she believed would signal to educators that I was there for a specific purpose: to learn, by hell or high water. And yes, Gloria was the hell and the high water.

By the time I was in first grade, Gloria had a whole

uniform planned for me even though no one at Sharon Elementary wore uniforms. She would take whatever small amount of money she had left over after handling the bills and we would go to Kmart, Marshalls, or TJ Maxx. She would buy six different polo shirts in six different colors, six different pairs of khaki shorts, and Birkenstocks, along with some oxfords and penny loafers. It was an intentionally preppy uniform that served as a visual cue to my teachers, saying, *This student is here to learn. Invest in her so that she can elevate to the highest level throughout her life.*

One day she heard through the grapevine that some of the students were getting half days because they had their *academic and gifted* testing time. She asked me if I'd completed the testing, but I had no clue what she was talking about. But because my mother knew how the world worked, having grown up under legally sanctioned segregation, she had a hunch that Black and brown students were being overlooked. (I told you she was the hell *and* the high water.) When she approached the school administrators, they promised to make a note for me to take the test the next year. But Gloria wasn't having it. As a result of my mother's intervention, I was eventually pulled out of class and given a Scantron test. The results came back days later, and Gloria was right: I tested off the charts, and thus I was able to enter Sharon Elementary's academically gifted program that year, just as some of my peers were doing. It was my first memory

of feeling seen in a school setting, of my academic potential being recognized. Getting into the program began a new
personal chapter for me, where I started to associate Blackness with achievement. No one could tell me that my experience, that what I would later deem to be my *Blackness*, was
inherently associated with mediocrity or underperformance.

Now, Gloria shouldn't have had to do any of that shit.
We all know that many white and Asian kids can show up
wearing ripped jeans and flip-flops and still receive maxi-
mum classroom attention and the presumption of academic
readiness. Therefore, my mother having to literally dress me
in a euro-white-mimicking uniform in order to better my
chances for a full academic opportunity wasn't just a damn
shame, it was literally anti-Black.

Autumn A. Arnett wrote a brilliant piece for the *Grio*
entitled "Black Brilliance Is Still Being Overlooked Because
White Systems of Education Don't Want to Change." She
is the executive director of the Brilliance, Excellence and
Equity Project, a national nonprofit organization that works
to achieve equity in gifted education through culturally
responsive teacher training. In her article, Arnett rightly
argues that while her children are enrolled in academically gifted classes because she possesses the luxury of time,
unique advocacy skills, and an unusual awareness of the
nuances of gifted systems and programs, most Black parents
don't share her positioning. She acknowledges that she is an

outlier. Arnett goes on to say that the systems and individuals who benefit from gifted programs don't actually want to change, and that putting the burden on Black parents to advocate on behalf of their children is immoral and in fact perpetuates the inequities some people claim they want to fix.

I agree with Arnett—full stop. And I agree with the disappointing yet unsurprising truth that she readily identifies—that education systems at gifted and talented programs in particular are anti-Black and will stay that way for the foreseeable future because the would-be change makers have no incentive to change these systems to properly include Black brilliance. So what do we do? We work around these assholes. And yes, in this context the system is an asshole. I unequivocally agree that what Gloria chose to do in order to ensure my academic access, just like what Arnett did for her children's academic opportunities, is what all Black parents must do in the current climate. And right now, all we have is the current climate. Yes, we should continue to fight for change within and around the system. We should demand that teachers do better by Black students and recognize our brilliance and academic potential for the gift that it is instead of condemning it as a disciplinary problem in need of punishment. But in the meantime, I'm not willing to sacrifice the brilliant Black babies who will be sidelined and silenced while we wait for centuries-old systems to change, particularly because we've seen little to zero evidence of the willingness of those who've benefited from these systems to do the work, endure the work, or make the space for past-due change. Therefore, I reiterate, in the meantime, when it comes to advocating for our children's education, let's all act like Gloria.

Even with my mother's strategies for accessing opportunity, she also knew that I would face prejudice at the school I was being bused to and that education in Black history there would be practically nonexistent. And so Gloria took it upon herself to supply me with a well-stocked library at home for the purpose of supplementing my school lessons. In our personal library, Black folks were placed front and center. In these narratives, I could lose myself in the stories of people who looked like me, who had experiences that helped shape or reflect my own experiences. From history books I got to learn about Black women trailblazers like writer Phyllis Wheatley and political leaders Barbara Jordan and Shirley Chisholm—pillars of excellence who're finally starting to make their way into the mainstream consciousness and who showcased to me what my future womanhood could look like. I also read novels by Mildred D. Taylor, whose writing is geared toward children, and as I got older books by Bebe Moore Campbell and Maya Angelou, whose writing is positioned toward adults.

It was also through my at-home library that I first learned

about Frederick Douglass, an iconic figure in the American consciousness for generations and the famed orator, writer, and government official tremendously pivotal in ending legal chattel slavery in the United States. As the most photographed person of the nineteenth century, his life has been widely deconstructed and chronicled. But as a kid, I was mostly fascinated by his intelligence and savviness, how he'd figured out that the key to emancipation was in education. As a youngster, he noticed enslaved people were forbidden to read and put two and two together, making it his mission to learn how to read through trickery and subterfuge. In my child's brain, I heard his genius conclusion as though he were whispering it to me directly: *Hmm, now if they don't want us to know how to read, there must be some deep power in reading. In knowing.*

BET ON BLACK MOVE

ALWAYS, I MEAN *ALWAYS* EXPAND YOUR CONSCIOUSNESS

For the sake of your own self-enlightenment and the sake of the young people in your life, you need to always be reading, whether it's historical works or self-help titles or fact-rich biographies or frothy commercial fiction or slim, serious sci-fi . . . really, whatever excites you. (I'm well aware

28

that I might be preaching to the choir here considering you're holding this book in your hands, but still, let me have my moment, especially for those of y'all who only read occasionally.) Study after study shows that reading sharpens your mind, broadens your imagination, and gives you access to language in a way that can't be mimicked by most other forms of entertainment. I believe this is why books—which are a pretty ancient form of media, if you think about it—remain a steadfast part of our culture. As I mentioned with Douglass, it's no coincidence that one of the most forbidden things an enslaved person could do was read. All sorts of horrible punishments could ensue from cruel enslavers for the daring act of expanding one's consciousness. A knowledgeable Black American is a deep threat to white supremacy.

As I craft this passage, I'm rereading *The 48 Laws of Power* by Robert Greene and W. E. B. Du Bois's *The Souls of Black Folk*, a quote from which graces the beginning of this chapter. And I recently reread James Baldwin's acclaimed essay collection *Notes of a Native Son*. In my mind, Baldwin is just absolutely essential to understanding how racism in America works, and his insights are offered via language that's invigorating and sublime.

All that to say, on the regular, sit your ass down and pick up a book.

BET ON BLACK

Being placed in advanced public school classes with a steady flow of Black history at home served me well, allowing me to fully inhabit the idea that being an excellent student was part of my racial identity. After Sharon Elementary, I attended Northwest School of Visual and Performing Arts during my middle school and high school years. It was far from being a cool school. There were no sports, no jocks or cheerleaders—a blasphemous, almost unthinkable setup considering Northwest was located in the South. We were just a bunch of geeky, artistic types trying to follow our passions and figure out who we were while doing the things that teens do. I became the free lunch kid who earned straight As, talked too much in class, and maintained a diverse group of friends. I was also into music, developing an abiding love for the individual careers of the two biggest Jackson siblings, Michael and Janet. In fact, "The Knowledge," the third song from Janet's classic 1989 album, *Rhythm Nation 1814*, proclaims over an industrial beat the importance of Black educational achievement.

Northwest, along with its emphasis on the arts, had high academic standards, and that was a good fit for me. Academics brought me joy. I loved my history and civics classes, reading about government and the Emancipation Proclamation and Reconstruction and the civil rights movement and the women's rights movement. Learning about revolution and change imparted by the will of the people was the single most gratifying experience I had as a teenager, along with immersing myself in a variety of narratives. My favorite books from high school were Elie Wiesel's Holocaust memoir *Night* along with the novels *Things Fall Apart* by Chinua Achebe and *Invisible Man* by Ralph Ellison.

When I read a text, no matter what it was, I felt like the pages contained an implicit invitation for my own commentary, prompting me to think about what I would do if I were in the shoes of the protagonist or narrator. But what was most thrilling to me was that I was seeing the experiences of Black people centered, and that I was able to discuss these texts with other students.

It was also in high school that I read what's considered the definitive book on Douglass's life, *Narrative of the Life of Frederick Douglass*. I was thus able to gain a deeper understanding of Douglass's radicalness, how courageous he was in daring to be defiant in myriad ways. He created space for himself in a world that had widely sanctioned his oppression. Though the circumstances of my upbringing were far less dire, it's the same spirit of defiance that informed my drive to seek opportunity after opportunity, to declare that my potential as a thinker and learner must be acknowledged and nurtured.

I graduated early from Northwest at sixteen, brimming with ideas, and soon left Charlotte to attend the University of North Carolina. There, I would continue down a path of centering Blackness. Though I knew I wanted to be an attorney, I also knew that I could major in whatever I wanted as an undergraduate as long as I eventually did well on my LSATs. And so I became a Black studies major. Learning about the richness of our community, something I'd done for years by this point, was far too compelling to give up.

BET ON BLACK MOVE

CENTER BLACKNESS FROM THE BEGINNING

Play around here. Make centering your history fun, eclectic, full of unexpected twists and turns. Using pop culture as a window into other aspects of life is always compelling and can serve as a sometimes subtle way of expanding your consciousness. Let's say you create a STEM-oriented weekend for the fam or friends, showcasing our contributions to the fields of science and technology. I know what you're thinking, but stay with me...Maybe you could watch an episode of the 1960s sci-fi series *Star Trek* with the late, great Nichelle Nichols as communications officer Lieutenant Nyota Uhura. You could then use that as a launching pad to discuss why her role as a supporting character was so groundbreaking for the time, going into the history of discrimination and how the civil rights movement arose in response. You could look into what Nichols achieved outside of the show, showcasing how she later worked as a spokesperson for NASA to recruit astronauts of color, and then you could jump into some intel on the first Black astronaut to fly into space, Guion S. Bluford. And then you could backtrack a bit and talk about the large group of Black women mathematicians who were integral participants in NASA's earlier programs starting in the 1940s, with Jim Crow still in effect, looking at the film *Hidden Figures*, which spotlighted the stories of Katherine G. Johnson, Dorothy Vaughan, and Mary Jackson. Or you can read the actual book *Hidden Figures* by Margot Lee Shetterly as a family, which would give a more accurate representation of the story of these women than the movie. Shetterly has written both a young readers' edition and picture-book version. Whichever version they read, your kids will still be learning about the broader culture while seeing themselves and those who came before them front and center in American history as opposed to being an afterthought in a narrative in which subordination and diminished possibility are expected.

Another suggestion: sit down and watch one of the screen adaptations of *A Raisin in the Sun*, the 1959 theatrical work by playwright Lorraine Hansberry. Maybe the 2008 Phylicia Rashad and Sean Combs version would be the one to view, as it has a more contemporary sheen than its predecessors. Even if your kids think this is going to be some dry-ass old people's shit from the last century, I suspect they'll get into the story once the drama picks up. Use the basic premise of the play, which centers on a family trying to move into an all-white neighborhood that doesn't want them there, to highlight how in the real world there were all sorts of discriminatory real estate policies that barred Black folks from moving into certain neighborhoods. In fact, Hansberry's father took this issue of restrictive real estate covenants to the Supreme Court and eventually won, though the process was arduous. Maybe show an article to your kids about this milestone. And none of this has to feel like homework with written assignments, even though research will be required for you as an adult in preparation; it just requires intention and an openness to discussion.

Dare to think outside the box in terms of how to center Black history. But whatever you do, take the time.

A lot of my later academic and professional achievements were based on the fact that, with my mother's insistence, I had bypassed a school system that didn't center Blackness. I mean, let's face it, Sharon Elementary didn't have my back. Okay, that's fucked up that I wasn't being fully supported in my development, but fine. At home, I was centered, as were the experiences of my people, and so the good news was that I was set up to thrive despite the white-centered curriculum I was force-fed at school. And trust me, most teachers and school administrators are *not* thinking they're delivering a white-centered curriculum to their students. They likely legitimately believe they're teaching our nation's history and experience as it happened . . . and that actually just happens to be white. See, on some level the erasure of Black American history and experience from our schools is unconsciona-ble, but most often our marginalization is a happenstantial by-product of basic white self-centeredness. Think about it: if *you* were in charge of telling a story or presenting an expe-rience, wouldn't it likely reflect the experience of you and yours? Exactly. So we're not giving out passes to white edu-cators for Black erasure in academic spaces.

Malcolm X once famously stated, "Only a fool would let his oppressor teach his children." This is proof that brother Malcolm understood. He understood that when you fully delegate the responsibility of educating and framing your child's identity to white institutions, you play yourself. I know you might cringe or be downright sad when I say this. You might think, *Well damn, when am I supposed to create and implement this supplemental Black-centered curriculum for my kids? I have a damn job!* But to keep it a buck, and to bor-row the sentiments of Malcolm, you better make time. Your own, your child's, and the culture's well-being depends on it.

To further highlight the dangers of allowing white-created school systems to educate our kids, let me break down a bit of recent history for y'all. The United States has been experiencing an unprecedented attack on the rights of public school students to have a comprehensive education. This attack is directly linked to the centuries-long subordination of Blackness that's existed in the country. According to the literary organization PEN America, between July 1, 2021, and March 31, 2022, more than 1,500 books were banned in dozens of school districts across twenty-six states. Organized by white Republican political leaders, conservative parents, and far-right agitators, these bans focused mostly on books that feature the LGBTQ+ community and Blackness.

It's galling to take note of some of the books that have been censored. The ban includes works like the acclaimed *All Boys Aren't Blue* by George M. Johnson, a captivating memoir focusing on the life of a Black queer boy, and the aforementioned *Bluest Eye*, by Toni Morrison. (In my resource guide at the end of *Bet on Black*, I have a full list of Black-oriented books that have been banned. Be sure to check it out.) Yes, the work of a Nobel Prize recipient who's considered one of the best writers to ever grace this planet has been banned in some school districts, which means that kids of all backgrounds, but most gallingly *Black* kids, may never experience her work if parents solely rely on school systems to control what their kids read. The idea that Black kids can readily feel like they have a place in this world, that their dreams and hopes and ancestral traumas can be recognized in the classroom, has become an even more endangered concept.

Though literary censorship has a long, sordid history in the states, PEN America has said that this assault on the First Amendment rights of students is particularly disturbing in terms of the swiftness and comprehensiveness with which the bans were implemented. Our high priestess of sound, Nina Simone, was known for her song "Backlash Blues," which she cowrote with Langston Hughes. In this groundbreaking song, she called out white people who pushed back against Black advancements made during the civil rights era. And that's exactly what these book bans are—a backlash against the embrace of the Black humanity, thought, and creativity we saw in the wake of the spring 2020 murder of George Floyd. Brother Floyd was an unarmed, nonhostile Black man who pleaded for his life as a white officer held his knee against Floyd's neck for almost ten minutes in Minneapolis, Minnesota. Everything was caught on video, available soon after to a national, captive audience, as so many of the distractions of modern life had been removed due to COVID-19 pandemic shutdowns. Folks were forced to be still, having no choice but to witness an unconscionable crime that symbolized the violence Black citizens have long endured in America.

Floyd's murder inspired a summer of unprecedented

global protests that dramatically changed the discourse over race. We also witnessed a flowering of Black expression in various media outlets, with the powers that be striving to atone for years of Black dehumanization. To be clear, bad-ass creativity has been a mainstay of the Black community for eons. The difference now was that the gatekeepers provided far more platforms for different types of Blackness. These gatekeepers wanted to place themselves on the right side of history and, in many cases, appeal to consumers who needed to believe they lived in an enlightened America. This embrace of our creativity sure enough extended to the world of literature. The *New York Times* best-seller lists were dominated by Black fiction and nonfiction titles for months, with folks of all backgrounds looking to understand racism more deeply or support Black and brown authors, who were now being pushed and pursued by publishers. And schools and libraries nationwide went out of their way to make sure the Black experience was prominently included on shelves and in curricula for their students.

But to those who have an investment in America's traditional power structure, who position their own value as being built on the backs of Black folks, such widespread change couldn't go unchecked. We've seen these moments time and time again in American history, most notably during the Reconstruction era, which saw an emergence of Black political power only to be followed by years of anti-Black terror and Jim Crow horror. In our current era, white conservative politicians have called out the dangers of so-called critical race theory in their campaigns while others have pushed for school districts to investigate books that they find problematic. These books often center on more accurate and nuanced representations of race than can be found in a standard textbook.

(Special note: Many conservative political leaders like to use the term "critical race theory" when describing Black history. This intentional rhetorical conflation is bullshit. It's designed to panic their base and spur them to action. Critical race theory actually consists of complex academic concepts created decades ago by legal scholar Kimberlé Crenshaw. Rest assured, our kids are *not* learning this. Instead, elementary, middle grade, and high school students are sometimes being offered books that feature general Black history or elements of the Black experience in fact, fiction, or poetry, as they should be.)

Thus multistate, multipronged book bans went into effect. In some cases, as seen in Florida, Republican-dominated legislative bodies were even able to pass laws that banned the discussion of Black history and racial awareness in classroom settings. Essentially, Black kids in Florida are forbidden from learning about who they are, from doing the very thing that Sturdivant has proclaimed is essential to our kids' self-esteem.

Are you thinking about the doll tests again? You should be.

I wanted to break all of this down for my readers so that y'all can get a sense of the inherent dangers of relying on traditional educational systems to do the right thing and center our history in the classroom. Though school districts with a predominantly Black and/or ethnically diverse population are much more likely to accurately present elements of the Black experience, such occurrences are by no means a given. And they're certainly not going to happen in predominantly white, conservative districts that want to continually center the so-called founding fathers—founding fathers who rampantly enslaved our ancestors, mind you—and portray America as a fair, racially equitable place.

While I know the realities of life dictate that most of us need to rely on the American school system to teach our kids and have relied on it to educate us about our history, there's no way we should assume that this system is going to accurately represent who we are, where we've been, and how we've lived. Ultimately, that work will be on us. That's why it's incumbent upon all Black people in America to make sure that we individually, and our kids, know the full breadth and depth of our history and experiences, that we go out of our way to center our experience in what we consume, whether it be books, TV, or other media.

This means that you need to take time to create an at-home curriculum focusing on Black experiences. And you sure enough need to make sure that books and other forms of media that you and the kids in your life are consuming outside of the classroom accurately reflect us.

Notice I keep saying "you and your kids." This is deliberate. Fact is, our children aren't the only ones with a tremendous and beautiful opportunity to learn and frame, or if need be, reframe Black American and African stories and experiences. The reality is that even at my age and with my fancy degrees, I am *still* learning about, processing, and advancing the framing of Blackness. So believe me, you too can derive enormous benefit from introducing or revisiting some of these Black primary and secondary sources. I have Du Bois's *The Souls of Black Folk*, Baldwin's *The Fire Next Time*, *The Autobiography of Malcolm X*, and Isabel Wilkerson's *Caste* on constant rotation on my personal reading list. While I've read them all several times, I visit these works again and again because each time I engage with them I get something new. Why? Not because I wasn't paying attention the first time, but because I'm a different woman, a different person, each time I consume their contents. *The Fire Next Time* lands differently now that I've lived in Harlem, USA for eight years. Same with Malcolm's autobiography. And *Caste* hits altogether different now that I've traveled the world and visited Yad Vashem: The World Holocaust Remembrance Center.

And I've got to add, please, *please* do not wait for Black

History Month to roll around to do this work of creating a curriculum. Yes, the origins of the month stemmed from the vibrant imagination of one of our own, scholar Carter G. Woodson. I get it, and God bless him for everything he did for us. But BHM is now being used by the larger society as a way of cramming all of our history into four weeks, the end, not to be dealt with for another year. Fuck that. Make sure our history is routinely front and center 365 days of the year.

If your kids attend a school system that happens to center our experiences, I'm thrilled for you, but frankly, most of us will have to do the extra work ourselves. And I say as a fellow adult that you should embrace the work, that you should embrace the enlightenment and awareness that will change your life as you're going over readings with the kids in your lives, learning new things about Black history that were never taught during our elementary school years. It's a damn shame it's taken this long, but it's never too late to grow and evolve.

Really, that's part of the good news of Blackness: now more than ever before, due to technology, we have ready access to our history via a wide array of sources, which enables us to do everything from getting advice on how to create a curriculum for kids to forming communities around Black history and learning as adults.

And I must reemphasize that it's not just about encouraging

our children to learn our history; it's also about making sure we do the same for ourselves as grown folk. That enrichment should be a regular part of our lives. Even with my Black studies degree, I continue to expand my consciousness all the time with the books, documentaries, podcasts, exhibits, and damn near everything that I can engage in in one way or another to educate myself on who we are. And I very much want for you to exult in who you know yourself to be based on the richness of a centered experience. I want all our kids to pick up Black dolls lovingly, as objects to be cherished, nourished, as symbols of our layered, worthy humanity.

CHAPTER 2

OPTICS

"The media is the most powerful entity on earth. They have the power to make the innocent guilty and to make the guilty innocent, and that's power. They control the minds of the masses."

—MALCOLM X

E VEN THOUGH I LOVED BEING A lawyer (and
I'd sure 'nuff spent enough years working my ass
off for my degree), the quote from Brother Malcolm speaks to why I chose to leave my career as
an attorney and go into the world of media as a broadcaster
and journalist—namely, I understood the overarching power
of representation in America.

I knew that in order to make the biggest difference in
the lives of others in my community, in order to reach as
many people as I could with my advocacy, I had to become
part of the world of media. When I first came across Malcolm's words, I felt in every fiber of my soul that I wanted to
manifest them in a way that would benefit Black folks on a

huge scale. I felt called upon to help transform the insanely narrow conversations about what Blackness is and will be. (There aren't many things I love more than the law, but being Black is definitely one of those things.) Through mass representation comes power, and I was very intentional in wanting to use my talents and skills to advance liberation.

Why do I love being Black so much? you might ask. Because it ain't for everybody. I've always had an affinity for the thing, the work, the benefit that comes with doing the thing that most folks, despite their best effort, cannot do. If it's a case anyone else can argue, I'm not interested. If it's a television role most people can successfully handle, miss me. I love being Black because it's an entirely unique experience that requires and allows individuality, grit, interpretation, and deliberate presentation. To put it mildly, there are a lot of people of color on this planet; we are indeed the global majority. Yet as Black folks, and as Black Americans specifically, we remain the most misunderstood racial construct in the world. Thus I love and am deeply appreciative of my ability to shape and fashion an exact, accurate, complicated, and challenging expression of Blackness.

America has presented distorted, vile images of Blackness for decades, whether via the live minstrel shows that dominated the nineteenth-century stage or Hollywood film depictions in which we were routinely seen as servants, buffoons, or savages. These tropes are an extension of the dehumanizing narratives that were used to justify our enslavement and subsequent placement in a system that viewed them as lower caste. When the transatlantic slave trade began in the sixteenth century, European enslavers dehumanized African natives and their descendants in order to justify the continual enslavement, mutilation, and murder of other human beings. After all, no reasonable, God-fearing person could commit such unspeakable acts to a fellow human being, so the dehumanization of Black Africans was necessary. And since Black humanity has never been sufficiently restored, this dehumanization has had a profound impact on how the world sees Black folks and how we see ourselves... *to this day.* Outside of the efforts of select Black leaders and a few of our allies, there's been no concerted, national effort to correct this dehumanization. And if Black people have been dehumanized and then never really rehumanized in the eyes of America, this means that we've been routinely fed stories that uphold our dehumanization in the collective imagination, especially via media.

But the joyous news for Black folks today is that all of us can actively participate in transforming the conversation around what Blackness is in terms of representation. You don't have to work in media to live out Malcolm X's truth. You get to have full autonomy over Black representation, whether you represent Blackness in person at work or virtually via social media. The liberation is in the choice, not

When it comes to representation, my first instructor on the power of optics, Frederick Douglass, once again showed us all how it should be done more than a hundred years ago. He became the most photographed person of the nineteenth century. Not the most photographed Black person, the most photographed person...period. This was by no means an accident. The writer and orator knew that he had access to platforms that other members of his community didn't have, and he wanted the world to see the face of someone who had once been enslaved, to see his humanity and dignity.

Look at the portrait of Douglass on the cover of David W. Blight's 2018 Pulitzer Prize–winning biography *Prophet of Freedom*. Your eyes will settle on the visage of a man who's physically beautiful, serious, determined, and regal, a man who would have been treated as less than human by most of the United States and shackled for life. Knowing this, Douglass purposely had so many pictures taken of himself to challenge the white people who would enslave Black people, to say to them via the power of his image: *If you can place someone like me in chains, with my beauty and austerity and poise, what does that say about YOU? What does that say about YOUR inhumanity, not mine?* On top of this, Douglass was also messaging to enslaved Black people with his image: *You are NOT what they say you are.*

Douglass's strategy for liberation would end up being echoed by another one of my teachers, James Baldwin. In the

1960s television program *The Negro and the American Promise*, Baldwin said, "What white people have to do is try and find out in their own hearts why it was necessary to have a nigger in the first place, because I'm not a nigger. I'm a man, but if you think I'm a nigger, it means you need it…If I'm not a nigger and you invented him—you, the white people, invented him—then you've got to find out why." And that's exactly what Douglass was aiming to highlight with his acts of portraiture, to represent Blackness in a way that forced white people to look at their need to dominate, to enslave, to dehumanize. Because that sure as hell ain't part of Blackness. That's not who we are.

BET ON BLACK MOVE

CRAFT YOUR REPRESENTATION WITH INTENTION

All of us now have the same powers of choice as Douglass in our frantic, social media–obsessed world, where the image we want to present to the world is only a selfie and a click of a button away. But amid the Instagram and Tik-Tok and BeReal of it all, along with legacy media forms like books, TV, and film, I think it's important to stop and ask yourself a really important question: how can you craft an image of yourself and your community that subverts the white gaze, that dispels these tired, trite notions of who we are as Black folks?

One example of political subversion that comes to mind for me immediately is the cover of the middle grade book *Black Boy Joy: 17 Stories Celebrating Black Boyhood*, which features a lovely portrait of a Black boy smiling as rendered by artist Kadir Nelson. And I understand the purpose of this art, to subvert a contemporary, prevalent notion that young Black men are undeserving or incapable of experiencing love, care, and happiness. It's useful for white supremacy to position Black boys' default modes of behavior as being centered around violence, hypermasculinity, and toughness. Namely, to say without saying it, *These Black boys ain't quite fully human.* This is a terrible lie that justifies subordinate positioning, denying Black boys the same opportunities as their white peers and endangering their very existence. And this is why I celebrate the *Black Boy Joy* images. Give me more. Why? Because research proves that somewhere between nine and twelve, these beautiful Black boys go from being perceived as cute little lovable American kids to being seen as scary, dangerous, violent threats. And if we're to do the necessary, life-saving work of protecting our Black boys and men, humanizing through Black boy joy images is a great place to start.

Before you post images or videos of yourself or others, whether for casual fun or work, sit with the media you're putting out into the world and see how you can create a narrative that showcases the full complexities of Blackness.

For the record, though I've stated that I was a Black studies major, the University of North Carolina at Chapel Hill called it the Department of African, African American, and Diaspora Studies, not using the term "Black studies" to describe coursework. I've never taken to the use of the term "African American." I think the phrase is a little anti-Black, actually, stemming from a time when people just weren't comfortable saying "Black" anymore. What I've noticed now is that in certain spaces, some people are still very uncomfortable with the term "Black," even though it includes far more communities across the globe and has far more poetic meaning than the term "African American." In fact, you'll find that I've chosen not to go deeply into exactly what Blackness is for the purposes of this book because I believe, outside of being of African descent in some way, that the elements of Blackness are way too varied, spectacular, and ineffable to be boxed in by a traditional definition.

And the sheer brilliance of Blackness was front and center when it came to the life teachers I was blessed to have, especially in college. As a sophomore at the University of North Carolina at Chapel Hill, I took one of the most transformative courses of my life. It was called Black Performance in Literature, and was taught by Professor Sonji Madison. Dr. Madison's diminutive stature belied what a magnificent force she was and still is in the classroom. Her command of language, insistence on bravery and truth-telling, and general integrity continue to be a major influence on how I approach my own work. In fact, she was also one of the first people who taught your Auntie E the power of sitting with the uncomfortable, a life philosophy I hold dear.

This notion of sitting with the uncomfortable is transformational. Frederick Douglass tells us, "Without struggle, there is no progress." I believe him. My lived experience tells me that only through the struggle do we obtain substantial, long-term change. As a person unwilling to accept that how things are or have been is how they have to always be, I'm committed to the necessary struggle and accompanying discomfort that we all must endure to progress.

At Chapel Hill, I was surrounded by enlightenment. The late Dr. Perry Hall, a professor who gave me Hillman College vibes from *A Different World*, taught Intro to African American and Diaspora Studies. He generally wore his hair in a slicked-back ponytail and sported a leather FUBU bomber jacket and hard-bottom leather dress shoes. Yes, that's how he came to teach, and we loved him for it.

For all the forcefulness that Dr. Madison had, Dr. Hall's instructional style was more casual, more chill, which often involved him sitting on his desk and talking to his students in a barbershop-style kind of way. He sometimes said things like, "Don't let class keep you from learning." He certainly wanted us to come to class, mind you, but he also understood that if the conversation on the yard was mentally stimulating where you needed to go spiritually and intellectually, stay on the yard. Well, he should've never told my Black ass that. I took his advice literally. There's been a part of me that's always been a facilitator of thought, even when I was a little kid on the playground. I do it with my friends, I do it on dates, I do it in my dreams…it's like breathing to me. Now I realize that I've always done this even though I wasn't as self-aware as a teen. I was constantly on the campus's main yard area at lunch, right by Lenoir Dining Hall. I would also sometimes stay up in the dining hall for hours holding court, sitting at a big round table with a rotation of friends and associates, discussing everything from geopolitical affairs to fashion branding to relationships. With Dr. Hall's words in mind, I realized that these interactions were my intellectual and emotional food, nourishment for my soul, and would in fact come to impact my future career in media.

Even though I appreciated wonderful teachers like Drs. Madison and Hall, the most impactful class I took at UNC by far was Black Representation in Television and Mass Media, taught by Dr. Charlene B. Regester. This class would have a profound effect on how I would go on to understand the power of media. Though we eventually covered every-thing from the Blaxpoitation era of the 1970s to progressive indie films, we started with early twentieth-century films that were disgustingly racist, including *Birth of a Nation* and *Gone with the Wind*. We discussed the irony of the latter movie being the first film for which a Black actress received an Academy Award. This was Hattie McDaniel, who won in the Supporting Actress category for her role as the enslaved woman Mammy. She gave a riveting, beautiful acceptance speech yet was made to sit in the back of the room apart from other cast members due to the segregationist Jim Crow laws of the day.

We also studied the 1954 film *Carmen Jones*, zeroing in on the titillating title character as played by Dorothy Dandridge. Contrasting Carmen with Hattie McDaniel's Mammy brought to light the two modes of existence Black women have found ourselves bound by, and thus Professor Regester spent a lot of time on this notion of Black wom-anhood being shackled by the contrasting archetypes of Mammy and Jezebel.

The Mammy was defined by her roundness, by her "aw shucks" happy-go-luckiness in being a servant and maternal figure to a whole bunch of white folks. The Jezebel, as rep-resented by the character of Carmen, is defined by her con-stant, all-consuming sexuality, finding fulfillment in flirting with and seducing men. Professor Regester asserted that these were the types of behaviors, as created by white people, that Black women were expected to follow in a larger society. Our usefulness was based on our ability to subscribe to the role of happy-go-lucky caretaker or submissive, lusty vamp.

For generations, Black women have been challenged by this duality of Mammy and Jezebel; a narrative not created by us has nonetheless become so pervasive in terms of how we're evaluated because of white supremacy. A Mammy's sole purpose is to exist for the sustenance of white comfort, to never have her own sexuality or agency—hell, to never even have her own family—to have a narrow range of speech that's all about coddling and consoling her charges. McDaniel, with all of her shuckin' and jivin' on-screen as Mammy in what some also see as a subversive performance, was actually a highly intelligent woman who led an elegant life in California, having been married several times in fact. The Mammy archetype doesn't allow for this reality.

When it comes to Black folks, the Jezebel isn't only seen as a seductress with a reckless sexual appetite, but she's also sometimes correlated with the tragic mulatto, that biracial and/or lighter-skinned Black woman who is positioned as an outsider in her own community. No other real identity construct is permitted for this sort of concubine. She exists, at least on-screen, primarily for the purpose of pleasuring white men or being an object of the white male gaze, and is seen as highly threatening to white women.

Examples of the Mammy stereotype appear in such television comedies as *Beulah* and *Gimme a Break*—centered on big Black women taking care of white families—along with the legion of films and other TV shows that have showcased Black women as maids with no indication that they had lives of their own outside of their service to white employers. The pancake syrup brand Aunt Jemima, with its image of a smiling Black woman in a red headscarf, is an example of the Mammy stereotype as well.

Examples of the Jezebel stereotype include all appearances made by Black women in the James Bond film franchise in the twentieth century, many of the appearances made by Black women in Blaxpoitation flicks, and the legion of video vixens who've appeared in R&B and hip-hop music videos throughout the '80s, '90s, and beyond. The music video examples are particularly important because they show how (mostly male) Black artists and creators can adopt and reinforce a racist, sexist archetype created by white people. Yes, it's sad to say, but Black people are fully capable of doing the work of white supremacy.

The Mammy-Jezebel binary has greatly impacted what Blackness can look like on the screen and in other forms of media representation, greatly influencing how we're perceived and treated in the larger world. And of course, there are damaging stereotypes that have been geared toward Black men: the Servant, as seen with the first Black film star,

Stepin Fetchit, who epitomized the concept of Black man as buffoon; the Brute, a characterization in which Black men are routinely seen as rapists and criminals, often used to legitimize acts of lynching; and the Mandingo, taken from the 1975 movie of the same name, with Black men being prized for their robust sexual prowess above all else.

I grew up with a group of women who—despite being gorgeous and having personalities that weren't particularly subservient or deferential to white folks—would have been automatically placed in the Mammy category because of their large body size. And I realized in retrospect that my mother, my aunt Sherri, and to a lesser extent my aunt Barbara, were actually trying to tell me that I would have access to parts of the world that weren't available to them because of how I looked, because I physically fit more the archetype of a Jezebel than a Mammy. My ability to move in the world in a way that would have been perceived as having less effort meant that maybe I could bring back some of the world's spoils for the fam. They pinned their hopes on my access to a variety of opportunities due to these notions of beauty that were problematic.

And they were far from alone. My aunts and the women in my family were simply carrying the water that was passed on to them from every single generation since our people landed on the shores of this land. Any Black-identifying person who could access white space for any reason possessed an opportunity to make American life better for themselves and those they loved. This is the root reason that some of our Black kinfolk with actual white appearance chose to pass in white society. Of course, passing is problematic. It's rooted in the need to circumvent the devastating effects of anti-Blackness. Yet so much of being Black in America is about figuring out when it's most strategic to create workarounds to anti-Blackness and assessing when we've acquired enough currency to blow up anti-Blackness in its entirety, leaving in its place the beauty and triumph of Black centeredness.

And yes, the concept of a Jezebel is inherently dangerous to Black women, to all of us, really. But at the same time it's not right for Black women to cut off our sexuality or expressions of desire for the sake of avoiding a toxic archetype.

Here's the issue: How do you preserve your ability to access and highlight your femininity and beauty and desirability while also bringing with you your complete substance—your intelligence and grit and assertiveness? And how do you not fall into the trap of Black respectability politics, of not curtailing your behavior to fall into suffocating notions of what it is to be a "dignified" Negro or acceptable Black woman?

Growing up I hadn't heard much dialogue taking on the Jezebel-Mammy duality, but what I heard in Dr. Regester's class was that there was a historically limited place for Black women in media. And if you tried to create more nuanced identities, there was reluctance and even hostility from both the powers that be and your own community. Variations on Black women representing anything other than the Jezebel-Mammy binary were met with accusations of "not really Black," "not Black enough," "acting white," or "unrealistic." The more I looked at these reactions, the more they made sense as effective ways to control and marginalize Black women in greater society. And the more I looked at these reactions, the more the binary revealed itself to be what it always was...bullshit.

I tried to unpack all of this as much as I could, talking about these concepts with other students and family and friends outside of UNC. Being in Dr. Regester's class provided me with the language and framework to put my inner-most feelings about Blackness into something that I could wrap my head around, something that I could go out into the world and speak about productively.

Moving beyond the Mammy-Jezebel binary would thus become supremely important to me, informing my career path and defining how I would show up wherever I went. I routinely push back on all energy that attempts to force my positioning into either end of the binary. If I'm a featured speaker for a professional event, I don't confine myself to ill-fitting suits, boxy tops, or other wardrobe choices that represent a fear of being too feminine or sexy. Likewise, I love how Lizzo so beautifully and boldly wears leotards and tights while playing the flute. It's such a perfect example of what's possible when a Black woman in America says "Fuck you" to the Mammy-Jezebel binary. Lizzo and so many Black women just like her are saying, "You're going to get *all* of this glamour, sexiness, and sophistication…and you're going to like it!" (It's worth noting that Lizzo and her team won an Emmy Award for her competition show *Watch Out for the Big Grrrls*.)

BET ON BLACK MOVE

DIVORCE YOURSELF FROM WHITE ACCEPTANCE

This bit of advice is particularly geared toward my sisters: in the same way that it's essential for all Black people to divorce ourselves from white acceptance, it's essential for Black women to divorce ourselves from the Mammy-Jezebel binary. Once you have an awareness that this construct is being thrust upon us in hopes that we'll pick a side, you don't have to pick a side. You don't have to subscribe to such a narrow binary. Take a breath, step back, and see what elements of life work for you. Go ahead and file for a complete divorce from this arbitrary standard of Black womanhood.

After going through all of that, it's also essential to honor who you know yourself to be even if it intersects with the Mammy-Jezebel binary in some way. You don't have to divorce yourself from your sexuality out of fear of being seen as hypersexual. Nor do you have to divorce yourself from your instinct to nurture or protect or provide for others because you're running away from a Mammy stereotype. You get to enter spaces freely and pick and choose and lean in and lean out to the extent that you want to, with an awareness that we all can embrace different archetypes at different times in complex ways.

At the end of the day, liberation is found in knowing that who you get to be is your choice. If you want to walk out here with your coochie cat out and rub your kitty nipples for everybody to see, I'm here for it, I really am, and no one should judge you for that. And if organizing your life around motherhood or being a professional caregiver for all creeds is your thing, no one should judge you for that either. If you're in fact a fusion of these sensibilities, awesome. You might even decide that there's almost nothing about the binary that's useful for you, that maybe a far more self-fulfilling archetype is about being a pro athlete or climate activist with a limited emphasis on caregiving or sexuality. Do you, sis, do you. Create your own hot mix and throw Mammy-Jezebel out the door.

I had unwittingly taken on the mantle of Black representation at a particularly young age, having absolutely no idea just how fraught this terrain was.

My mother, with her perennially striving spirit, enrolled me in an obnoxious number of extracurricular activities when I was a kid, including ballet and piano classes via scholarships, modeling, and acting. At the age of six, I was signed to the Jan Thompson Agency in Charlotte. I did a lot of commercials for everything from Piggly Wiggly grocery stores to Kmart while also auditioning for big-time movies, including *Fried Green Tomatoes*. I even once auditioned for the film *Interview with a Vampire*. In the book, the girl is Creole, so that's what casting agents were calling for. I'm of Creole descent, but looking back at old pictures, I don't necessarily believe I would read as Creole. But my determined mother was like, "Fuck that, you're going to go on this audition." And I eventually got two callbacks, even though the role ultimately went to Kirsten Dunst, who was a full-on white girl. That was straight out of the book of Gloria.

In fact, if my mother were to write a self-help book, the first line would be, "We don't care what people are asking for—we're going to show them what they need!" This attitude of being unwilling to wait for someone else to decide what they want (which invariably means your opportunity will be contingent on their timetable and their demands) is critical to sustainable success. I use this approach often, and I suggest you adopt it as well. I sometimes call it the Steve Jobs approach. Think about it. Did you ever ask for an iPhone? Do you know a single person decades ago who decided they

And of course, we know it wasn't just me. We, the culture, recognize when white Hollywood rewards the Jezebel casting of Halle Berry in *Monster's Ball* and the Mammy castings of Viola Davis and Octavia Spencer in *The Help*. Those Academy Award wins and nominations weren't random. All three of those actresses have played a litany of brilliant, complicated Black characters throughout their careers. But the industry does its best to keep us in our place. They use Oscars, Grammy awards, and big checks to do the gatekeeping, which is why it's so necessary that we divorce ourselves from codependency on the shiny things to affirm our choices and positioning. I'm not saying we shouldn't get our proper pay or even collect some well-deserved hardware, but we should be observant and skeptical of how those in power seduce and reinforce their will. And this advice applies to all sectors of your life, including your workplace and geographical community.

I also experienced gatekeeping as a child in another form of mass entertainment—beauty pageants. Yes, as a kid, I also participated in pageants. One afternoon, as my grandmother picked me up from ballet class, an older white woman named Clara stopped us. Ms. Clara was the grandmother of one of my ballet classmates and thought I should enter a beauty pageant, and handed my grandmother a pamphlet for the Miss Cinderella Girl competition. My grandmother took the pamphlet home and immediately repeated to my mother what Ms. Clara had announced. The problematic, objectifying ideals spurred on by the beauty industry didn't matter to Gloria. She quickly agreed that I should compete, seeing college scholarships and other financial awards in my future, with dreams dancing in her head that I would eventually be the next Miss Teen USA.

And so I embarked on my pageant career. I won some local titles and eventually made it to the Miss Cinderella North Carolina State Pageant. I was so excited, winning the talent and personality prizes and coming in as first runner-up for the overall competition, holding hands with another little Black girl, who would be the winner. It was a scandal that night that the two top contestants were Black American. I remember walking out of the hall with my first-runner-up trophy and hearing the peanut gallery of white adults fuming, uttering comments like, "I can't believe this." "That was crap!" "This was rigged." And more trashy whoop-de-doo. The moment was both celebratory and fraught, becoming one of the first times when I understood firsthand that there were people who didn't want me to succeed based on the color of my skin.

(The pageant industry is a more acceptable part of life in the South compared to the North, and in many ways it was a nice fit for my personality. Now I know some of y'all are reading this and rolling your eyes at the mere mention of the pageant industry. I feel you. Yet, I invite you to consider that liberation is rooted in choice. So if one wants to flaunt their well-toned ass in a swimsuit and then crush a geo-political onstage interview question while wearing a crys-tal evening gown, then that's their choice. And if they use a platform originally designed to exploit and limit expec-tations of women and flip the paradigm to empower and advance a pro-women's agenda, all while refining their own public speaking and presentation skills, even better.)

From almost as early as I can remember, I'd been fasci-nated by concepts and constructs of Black beauty, which as a girl spurred my interest in collecting Black Barbies and Cab-bage Patch Kids. This interest was particularly encouraged by my grandmother, who was into glamourous aesthetics, and my aunt Sherry, a stunning, voluptuous woman. One of my favorite memories from my childhood consisted of our annual attendance at the Ebony Fashion Fair shows when they came to North Carolina. The fashion fair, helmed by Eunice Johnson and connected to the publication *Ebony*, was a series of popular runway shows that traveled the country for decades starting in 1958. Seeing gorgeous Black women of various hues and sizes in haute couture gowns that I would never otherwise see in North Carolina was such an enriching ritual. Coupled with my Black-oriented personal library, the fashion fairs gifted me with the message *You are of worth . . . you can be a person of glamour and prestige . . . you . . . can . . . shine.* I wasn't receiving this message from the larger world, certainly not when I attended Sharon Elementary and not when I went on my modeling and acting casting calls.

BET ON BLACK MOVE

CREATE BLACK-CENTERED RITUALS

It's a no-brainer that as Black folks, we should go out of our way to support Black cultural institutions and artistic endeavors. That means everything from spending a full day at the National Museum of African American History and Culture in DC to attending concert dance performances put on by the likes of Alvin Ailey and Dallas Black Dance Theatre. Creating ritual around these events and forms of expression is important, much in the same way that many Black Texans have done for generations with Juneteenth way before it became a national holiday, and like other folks have done with the Essence Festival of Culture in New Orleans every year. Creating rituals is important because it gives us a sense of order and completion in what can otherwise feel like a chaotic life. Like my aunt did with the Ebony Fashion Fair, can you locate Black cultural events that you can create rituals around for yourself, for your family and friends?

Keep in mind it's just as important to support and create rituals for cultural expressions that may not technically be Black events but still manage to center Blackness. Let's take the case of my girl Vanessa Williams during one of her runs on Broadway. In 1994, Vanessa Williams joined the cast of the Broadway musical *Kiss of the Spider Woman*. Her starring in the show revitalized box office ticket sales because tons of Black theatergoers decided to go see our girl. The musical's premise—two men imprisoned in Argentina dreaming of a legendary musical performer—wouldn't be positioned by most Black Americans as part of our collective experience. But Vanessa Williams is a member of our community, and folks sure enough did the right thing by showing up for her. (Critics and general audiences alike said she totally kicked ass in the role, by the way.) By showing up, we supported a member of the community and gave Broadway the message that our dollar needs to be respected, that we'll support projects where we deservingly see ourselves as stars.

We should approach the career of ballerina Misty Copeland in the same way. Copeland is an acclaimed performer who, despite not receiving dance training in early childhood like most ballerinas, became the first Black woman principal dancer for American Ballet Theatre. And she did this while having a body type—strong, athletic, beautifully muscular—that isn't seen as the norm for the ballet world, where skinny, swan-necked white girls have fluttered and pecked around wispily for centuries. Copeland's ascension

means that Black folks need to take our asses to the ballet if her company is in town and she's performing. Yes,
it means when Copeland is on the bill, we're supporting
the likes of American Ballet Theatre, which has focused on
primarily European dance forms, in the same way that we
would more unequivocally support Alvin Ailey, which is a
predominantly Black dance company founded by a Black—
and queer—choreographer. In the same way that supporting a completely Black-centric experience is important, it's
also important to create ritual around a Black person literally taking up space and being centered in venues not
created for us. We then send institutions the message that
we can be anywhere and everywhere we damn well please,
and I don't know what's more Bet on Black than that.

Blackness has been routinely policed by the white imagination in a way that I wasn't able to fully grasp during some
of my earlier life experiences. As a kid, I was told by white
arbiters of culture that I wasn't the right type of Black girl
for whatever project I was auditioning for, that I needed to
be more edgy, more urban. I didn't fit the narrow concept
of Blackness they were trying to sell for their project. I was
expected to conform or expect rejection. I mean, it was
fuckin' insane for a kid to experience. Why isn't authentic, expansive Blackness treated with the respect it deserves?

Why has it taken so long for white gatekeepers to create space for the preppy Black girl, or the geeky, inquisitive Black girl, or the cutesy-kid-next-door Black girl? Now, y'all remember Baldwin's earlier quote about how the white imagination needs Black people to be subordinate?

All of the archetypes I've presented here are an authentic part of Blackness and are roles that could have readily filled Hollywood screens for the last century if those in power had any investment in a rich, expansive Black experience. And my experiences as a kid along with countless others speak to why it's so fuckin' dangerous to allow white people to call the shots when it comes to our representation.

During my time at UNC, I learned another concept that drives me to this day—that representing Blackness in a media space comes with a huge responsibility because we have such low representation on the airwaves and the screen due to racism. In a historical sense, we literally don't have the privilege of abundant representation. Thus the few of us who get to represent Blackness in a mainstream media landscape have a lot to contend with, doing a heavy lift in terms of all that we bring to the table. Professor Regester gave an example to me about this that related to bombshell Pamela Anderson. She explained that Pamela Anderson gets to be Pamela Anderson in all her seminude glory without having to shoulder the responsibility of personally informing broader understandings of white womanhood. This is because, comparatively, there are tons of white women represented in media. Pam Anderson can be whatever she wants to be, receiving less judgment from the masses—even for the more supposedly scandalous parts of her public life—because there are countless other white women public figures like Madeleine Albright and Nancy Pelosi and Jessica Chastain and Katie Couric and Maria Shriver and Joni Mitchell and Judy Chicago and Patti Smith and Margaret Atwood, and the list goes on and on and on. Look at how Pamela Anderson's career managed to survive the release of her mid-'90s sex tape with then husband Tommy Lee, with Anderson starring in her own syndicated TV show for years afterward. Compare this to the professional cancellation effort that my girl Janet Jackson weathered after her Super Bowl wardrobe malfunction.

The abundance of white representation allows for more freedom among white individuals. When you don't have that abundance of representation, which of course Black folks haven't really had since the creation of television, the expectation of what you are representing is different. Look at the firestorm that confronted Viola Davis and Octavia Spencer for their roles in *The Help*. They were castigated for playing women who were domestics, seen as a continuation of the types of subservient—can we say Mammy?—roles that Black women were relegated to for decades in twentieth-century Hollywood. As I noted earlier, Hollywood may have rewarded these women for playing such roles, but many people in the Black community would have none of it.

Davis, our anointed Woman King as of the 2022 hit film with the same name, has gone on to say she regrets taking on her role in *The Help* even though it earned her an Academy Award nomination. And this connects to another important point: when you have the responsibility of representing the collective, of being at the vanguard of moving the collective forward, as empowering as that can be in some ways, you literally don't get to be an individual in your representation.

Look at the case of actress Nichelle Nichols. As I mentioned in the previous chapter, most of the world knows her for her work as Lieutenant Uhura on the original *Star Trek* series from the 1960s and the subsequent films of the '80s and '90s. Nichols at one point wanted to quit the show, seeing that her screentime was being reduced, to pursue a career on Broadway as a singer and dancer. (Yes, Uhura could get down with movement and vocalize.) But Dr. Martin Luther King Jr. asked her to stay. He saw her presence on a trailblazing television show as quite important to the civil rights movement and millions of young people. Nichols seemed to have made peace with her decision in subsequent years and loved being this type of icon, but did she ultimately sacrifice her own personal agency for the sake of other Black people, for the sake of the collective? This is the dilemma that continually pops up when a group's full range of experiences is insufficiently, woefully represented in the larger culture. This is in fact the dilemma that would pop up for me.

The burden of representation remained extremely relevant to me as I became a media professional after working for years as an attorney. This was around 2010. At the time of my career transition, I thought there was some very good representation of Black women in the media, though it was significantly more limited than what we have now. This was the pre-*Scandal* era, before audiences had Kerry Washington's portrayal of Olivia Pope. Melissa Harris-Perry was one of the few Black cable news hosts in the entire landscape, and Tamron Hall was on NBC and *The Today Show* as a headliner. Beyoncé and Rihanna ruled the R&B/pop/dance firmament, and Halle Berry continued to work it as a Hollywood contender. And, of course, the legacy of Oprah Winfrey's talk show was still floating in the public consciousness as it was soon about to end in 2011. Perhaps most important, Michelle Obama had entered the White House, iridescently redefining who and what the American First Lady could be. All that to say, we were certainly starting to see powerful representation in different quadrants of our media universe, but it was still very new, still relatively limited.

The TV media landscape was also dominated at the time by reality shows like *Basketball Wives*, *Love & Hip Hop*, *Braxton Family Values*, and *The Real Housewives of Atlanta*, which presented particular tropes around who Black women were.

That was the preferred way that platform gatekeepers wanted to present Black women on the small screen. And I in fact have no problem with that, that there's a power to be found in these women's experiences, that *Atlanta* Housewife NeNe Leakes or the Braxton sisters are quite important in terms of how they portray their experiences to the larger world via reality TV. That's a part of our liberation, to unadulteratedly express ourselves for the masses as we see fit without carrying the burden of respectability politics. But the conundrum was that we still had such low comparative representation of Black women on TV that the cultural weight of the portrayals on these reality shows was significant. These depictions erroneously ended up being seen as the sum total of who Black women are.

By the early 2010s, I was very clear that I would enter the media arena. I was constantly being mindful of how I could broaden the conversation about who Black women are—really, about who Black *people* are—while being true to my history and innate interests. If I wanted to represent something other than what I was seeing on certain platforms, other than the tropes and limited perceptions and stereotypes of Black women, getting away from the Mammy-Jezebel binary, then my attitude needed to be like, *Bitch, get into the arena*, and participate in the broadening of what Black women look like in mass media.

My media journey started with radio and then TV news,

where I landed at CBS and then Fox News. I didn't realize that an undergraduate class would have such a consequential, long-term impact on my career, helping to inform how I approached my image as an on-air personality. And I went on to be successful at much of what I did, but I made big mistakes as well.

During my Fox News days, I was wholly preoccupied with my responsibility to be what I perceived as a "good" representation of Black people and Black women on the network while receiving pushback from some members of the Black community for being on Fox in the first place. The pressure was nonstop, and I struggled with depression. I got criticized everywhere. On Facebook, on Twitter, on the NYC subway, at the grocery store...everywhere.

I eventually sought out therapy, which proved to be immensely helpful. At one point my therapist was just like, "At what point do you stop representing the culture and get to actually *participate* in the culture? At what point do you get to actually just be Eboni?" It took me a while to figure out how to do that, how to continue my walk and be of service to others as an on-air personality and advocate while also taking lots of time to do the things I needed to do for myself.

I know I'm not alone with this type of struggle. Dana Canedy was the first Black publisher for the Simon & Schuster imprint, and, after only two years, decided to resign. And she did so to carve out time to write a follow-up to her memoir *A Journal for Jordan*. "The issue when you're 'the first' or 'the only,' is that to many, you represent an entire industry," she said to the *New York Times*. "And I embrace that. However, it made it harder to make a decision that I felt was right for me." And I thoroughly, thoroughly connected to her sentiments here. I'm extremely passionate about the importance of Black representation, but I've learned over time that you need to balance your ability to serve the collective in a way that still feels like you're honoring who you know yourself to be and your personal comfort. Once the scales tip the other way, where you're sacrificing your health in the name of representation, it goes to where I was when I worked at Fox. I was no longer operating from a place of liberation. One shouldn't ever prioritize the responsibility of representing Blackness at the risk of one's own well-being.

Sometime after leaving Fox, I unexpectedly joined the cast of *Real Housewives of New York*. I never would have thought I would do reality TV for all the reasons I previously outlined—that it was too dramatic, that the shows were interested in a particular kind of Black female expression— but then it felt like God was really kind of winking at me with the sentiment, *Okay, now I'm going to bring this particular kind of opportunity to you*. If I really, really was about that life, you know, it meant jumping into a certain type of arena that wasn't made with ideas of Black excellence and expansiveness in mind. There's a certain type of viewer who gravitates toward news channels versus those who consume reality TV, whose conception of narratives about Black womanhood might be seen as narrower and clichéd. And that helped inform my decision to enter this type of TV landscape and do *RHONY* with a certain aesthetic sensibility and with a view toward presenting particular types of messaging that centered Blackness. My decision exemplified Professor Madison's idea of sitting with the uncomfortable. I could embark on a course of action that was challenging to parse through but fulfilling in terms of my personal mission of promoting Black awareness.

By the time I was on *RHONY*, I felt less pressure to get the representation dilemma right, so to speak, and I was far more invested in presenting what I knew to be my own truth and the truth of my people. When the *RHONY* opportunity showed up, I'd realized that there was no "right" way to represent Blackness or Black women. The concept itself is problematic and only does the work of reinforcing the binaries and mechanisms that are used to control Black women. I knew that I only needed to be my complete and authentic self...that was the only *right* approach I concerned myself with.

I made my debut as a *RHONY* cast member during the show's thirteenth season, the first Black woman selected for such a role on the infamous reality TV series. After experiencing the great personal cost of not centering Blackness in other spaces, I'd become insistent on the centering of my people and history in *all* spaces. I planned the eighth episode of the season, which would ultimately be dubbed "Harlem Night," spotlighting one of the most storied neighborhoods in America. When I was brought onto the show, I expected that I would be the gatekeeper who would show most of my castmates my Harlem...our Harlem...for the first time. It was an aesthetically beautiful telecast, with an emphasis on multifaceted glamour and elegance. I sported a gold Gucci bodysuit with a buttery-soft pencil skirt from St. John, literally allowing my body to be gilded. My feet were clad in classic So Kate stilettos from Christian Louboutin and my hair was slicked back in a long, sleek ponytail, accentuated by flawless makeup. The note I gave to my brilliant makeup artist was, "Think Beverly Johnson's *Vogue* debut cover glam." A humble homage to a trailblazing sister who'd come before.

The event was hosted at the renowned West Harlem eatery B Squared, owned by a queer Black woman. The space also happened to house the only speakeasy that still exists in the neighborhood. The dining area was full of gardenias, almost as if you were stepping into Billie Holiday's dressing room. A Latinx band performed live music, suffusing the space with the sounds of jazz legends like Sarah Vaughan and Charlie Parker. And the downstairs area looked like you'd walked into the den of Josephine Baker, offering plush, velvet-tufted love seats, golden mirrors, a wooden bar, and

RHONY episode set in Harlem after thirteen years. Yet after the episode aired, a critic from the website *Vulture* who regularly gives rundowns of *RHONY* episodes took me to task for not playing into basic reality TV tropes, which generally consist of spectacle for the sake of spectacle and tomfoolery to satiate a particularly toxic type of viewership. I understand as a media personality that criticism of what I put out there is to be expected, and in fact I would have welcomed an analysis of what I'd curated. But that wasn't the case. I was completely taken aback to read this writer's specific critique of me as not engaging in sufficient fun and games for the *RHONY* franchise. They claimed to be bored. Thus I was labeled a bad Housewife and bad entertainer because of my audacity to go against the grain and show something relevant to Black culture and who I am at my core.

I wanted to throw the whole write-up at the wall. Too bad the shit was digital. I thought it was so lazy, and indicative of a state of mind disinterested in Blackness. The writer, who could certainly be deemed a cultural gatekeeper, wasn't ready to engage with an episode that focused on Blackness not as a trauma story or a source of shuckin' and jivin' but as a place of unadulterated excellence, elegance, and iconography. I soon noticed that other online feedback seemed to mirror this particular writer's criticisms. Viewers wanted to see me, as the first *RHONY* Black Housewife, engaging in the standard reality TV hair pulling and salad tossing and

wine throwing and cussing out. There was a distorted out-
cry for me to resort to behaviors that would have served as
a modern-day example of minstrelsy, hearkening back to a
time when my worth would've been measured by how well
I could be the buffoon, all so white folks could feel better
about themselves.

Well, I'm happy to say, I'm simply not here for that.

I made a very conscious decision not to subscribe to what
some folks wanted, providing instead what I thought they
needed. People assumed I didn't understand the reality TV
assignment of drama for drama's sake, adhering to particular tastes. But I in fact saw the assignment, read it, and tore
it up. It would not have served my own personal liberation,
the liberation of my people, or the broader culture's liberation to do more of the same.

I crafted an online article responding to the *Vulture* critic,
making it clear where I was coming from. While writing, I
couldn't help but think back to earlier times in my life when
I'd put on a brave face while questioning what type of spaces
I could occupy and undermining myself. But now I know it's
my responsibility to seize the opportunity to define Blackness on my own terms in every room I'm in. I've learned I
am in no way obligated to engage with the terms that have
been expected of or presented to me, and neither are you.

Even after doing things my way on *RHONY*, I'm still
not fully comfortable making rigid qualitative judgments

about our media landscape. But I can say quantitatively that there's much more diversity in the range of Black experiences presented today than what I observed when I first entered the scene. I maintain that the diversity we see now is the result of the push that many Black media folks have made to occupy space, taking advantage of the opportunities that arose from having multiple streaming platforms and programming targeted to specific audiences. Seeing Joy-Ann Reid, the first Black woman to have a prime-time cable news show as a solo host, is very important. Seeing Lena Waithe, a queer, out, and proud Black woman representing relationships between women on *Master of None* and creating shows like *The Chi* and *Twenties*, is wonderful. And in the reality TV sphere there's progress as well, looking at the nuanced diversity of the cast of *The Real Housewives of Potomac* and *The Real Housewives of Salt Lake City*, for instance, or a show like *Married to Medicine*. Seeing a whole show built on the premise of Black women physicians is very important. As with any reality show, one could critique certain aspects of these series, but the premise of each of them is revolutionary and freeing.

Part of the good news about being Black today is that finally, after decades of limited, stultifying representation, we're finally entering an age in which we're starting to see a wide range of Black representation in various fields.

In the space of television, Black audiences might in fact

find themselves unable to watch all of the shows currently available that feature our experiences in nuanced, fresh ways. Still, it's our duty to intentionally, routinely cultivate a viewing schedule that prioritizes the shows where we're primary players. This is especially important when considering the online pushback and vitriolic trolling over the centering of Black representation in TV series and films that had previously tended to center whiteness, such as the Star Wars, Star Trek, and Lord of the Rings franchises as well as *House of the Dragon* and the remake of *The Little Mermaid*. (I mean, God forbid that Wonder Woman is ever cast as a super-fly sister...)

So let's take the time to do the research to discover what TV series and films are Black produced, in addition to having Black stars. Let's delight in Quinta Brunson's *Abbott Elementary*, and Issa Rae's *Insecure*, and Robin Thede's *A Black Lady Sketch Show*, and Bashir Salahuddin and Diallo Riddle's *Sherman's Showcase*, and Michaela Coel's *I May Destroy You*. And let's delight in the varied accomplishments of film directors and producers like Jordan Peele and Gina Prince-Bythewood and Ava DuVernay with their collective body of work that includes gems like *Get Out*, *Beyond the Lights*, and *Selma*. If a screen project isn't technically coming from Black creators, then let's make sure that they're doing damn right by our history and centering Blackness in a truly creative, nonexploitative way. This was seen with another Regina

King project, *Watchmen*, an Emmy-winning limited series that's supposed to be about superheroes but is in fact an astoundingly deep meditation on racial trauma associated with the 1921 Tulsa Race Massacre. Keeping in mind that some shows might be misses, that you won't enjoy them as much as you would've liked, it's nonetheless essential to always have Black TV series and films as part of your viewing lineup, boosting ratings, of course, and providing opportunities for discourse on social media.

Looking at the media of today, you not only have a legitimately diverse array of programs to choose from, but, on your own social channels, you get to be who you want to be, whenever you want to be, however you want to be. You have full choice in deciding how to make your own personal contribution to Blackness, and I guarantee that someone out there will applaud your move, feel seen, and share the love. So kick those damn binaries to the curb. Stomp out white cultural gatekeeping, and let's continue expanding Blackness in all arenas of representation. Let's do our damnedest to control our optics all the time, at every level.

CHAPTER 3
DISRUPTION

"Power concedes nothing without a demand...The limits of tyrants are prescribed by the endurance of those whom they oppress."

—FREDERICK DOUGLASS

no shame, and with a willingness to bear the consequences of our demand.

We have to understand that the reactions to our demands aren't always going to be pleasant, that articulating what we want will in fact come with a cost. But nonetheless, I maintain that if we're looking for consistent empowerment as a community, we have to dare to demand any and everything we want at the highest level, whether it's in the arenas of economic power, political leadership, or, as we just discussed in the previous chapter, representation.

Our Blackness is powerful. Our experiences are valuable, and they can be an astoundingly effective disruptor of white expectation. This concept of disruption, of shaking up the status quo in some way, has been one that's near and dear to my heart for some time, informing how I approached my life as a Black woman and professional. Any time there's Black existence beyond the confines of white designation, we have a disruption, and I am a perennial disruptor. Before I go on, though, it's also important for me to proclaim here that I'm a child of God, and I position my faith as a cornerstone of my ability to endure hard times. I don't think I could view my personal identity, my Blackness, or the way in which I move through the world without having that innate relationship with my God. I feel very called to do the work that I do and very called to occupy particular spaces, which has informed the type of connections I forge and how I show up.

One could argue that my entire career has been informed by this concept of grappling with spaces that weren't designed for me, and I imagine that it could be the same for you.

As mentioned in the previous chapter, becoming a Housewife was the farthest thing from my mind in terms of my career trajectory. Though I enjoyed several shows, I just didn't think that I would be a particularly good fit for a franchise known for casting a whole bunch of women notorious for drunken shenanigans, screaming at each other over the most trifling things, and woeful, privileged ignorance. But, when I heard that *RHONY* was specifically looking for a Black woman, as I've mentioned, I decided to take the conversation and see what opportunities might be there. At the start of the screening process, I was engaged to be married and so could have been considered a type of working Housewife, I suppose, but that relationship ended before I was selected. Nonetheless, the Bravo TV producers didn't see the end of the engagement as a problem, and after a months-long screening process, I got the call.

It was autumn 2020 and the COVID pandemic had hit the United States only months before, and so I was self-isolating, working at my home studio and recording for *REVOLT Black News.* A number I didn't recognize from an incoming call kept on popping up on my phone while I was recording. Once I wrapped, I quickly called the number back to see who this was. The woman who answered was like,

"Hi, this is Lisa Shannon. I'm the head of Shed Media...I'm calling to tell you that we think you would be the perfect addition to our new season of *The Real Housewives of New York City*, and we'd love to make you an offer."

Inside I reeled and gushed and couldn't quite believe my ears, but I kept the conversation professional and relatively short. "Fantastic!" I said. "Very much looking forward to speaking with you soon and figuring out the terms of the offer."

After we chatted a bit more, I hung up and danced a little dance because I was like, "I'm going to be a fucking Housewife! This is insane!" I'd been watching these bitches for sixteen years and I was soon going to be standing up there on-screen with an apple and my own tagline. My previous ambivalence about potentially being on the show was nowhere to be found. I just sat in bliss for a minute, thinking, *This is fucking unbelievable. And very, very cool.* I realized that, as much as I might've fought it, there was something about the Housewives aesthetic that spoke to who I am. I also began to put two and two together and predicted that this was going to totally elevate my career.

By the time I'd been told I would be on the show, the world had changed as well. We weren't only living through the first year of the COVID pandemic and the accompanying social changes and traumas, but we had lived through a summer of unprecedented global protests after the murder of George Floyd. It was a rhetorical, racial reckoning that my generation had never experienced. And the murder of Brother Floyd and the uprising that followed affected me deeply. I thought about what would be my responsibility to my community and myself once I started working on the *RHONY* set.

My need to disrupt rose to the fore once again. I immediately knew that I would be part of the movement to hold our nation accountable for making sure that the newly established terms of engagement about race after Floyd's murder were met consistently. And I would be really sticking to those terms of engagement, regardless of what was considered the norm for the Housewives franchise.

Still, there were challenges to contend with. When I was announced as the first Black cast member of *RHONY* in October 2020, the decision was celebrated as an about-time move. But, once again, I was also met with criticism. Story of my life. Some critiques came from the Black community via social media or the comments section of articles sharing the announcement. Folks wrote things like "Is she even Black? You know, she doesn't necessarily look Black to me. She looks biracial. She looks South Asian to me. She doesn't look like a 'normal' Black woman...a real sister."

So please allow me to tangentially venture into territory that I've been aware of for most of my life yet have not deeply dealt with so far in this book. I think my community is right to say if I didn't hold this aesthetic that's somewhat palatable to mainstream white audiences, I wouldn't be where I am today. I have indeed benefited from what some might see as a white-proximate aesthetic, but this has in no way meant that I don't happily, exuberantly identify as Black, and that I haven't used my privilege to serve as a disruptor in anti-Black spaces.

Favoring lighter-skinned Black people over darker-skinned members of the community is called "colorism." There's the definition of colorism that iconic author and activist Alice Walker first gave to us in 1983 in an essay in her book *In Search of Our Mothers' Gardens*, which is "prejudicial or preferential treatment of same-race people based solely on their color." Then there's the very academic definition presented by the National Conference for Community and Justice: "a practice of discrimination by which those with lighter skin are treated more favorably than those with darker skin. This practice is a product of racism in that it upholds the white standards of beauty and benefits white people in the institutions of oppression (media, medical world, etc.)."

Though I've been referred to as light skinned by many, and thus a beneficiary of colorism in terms of what opportunities were made available to me, I've also sometimes been considered the darker girl in certain circles. When I met Creole students at Loyola Law School or when I'm in certain parts of Europe, I'm immediately positioned as darker skinned by some. That sense of relativity has stayed with me. While doing *RHONY* promotions, I once appeared on the talk show *ZIWE* on an entire episode about beauty standards. There was an interesting part of the conversation when the host, Ziwe—who would be considered by many to be a dark-skinned Black woman—called me "light skinned," and my knee-jerk reaction was almost to push back on that. I've come to realize there's no such thing as light skinned or dark skinned. There's only *lighter* skinned and *darker* skinned because skin color is always viewed in relation to whom you're engaging with. If I'm in conversation with, say, Soledad O'Brien, another woman of color, I become darker skinned to people.

No matter where you fall on the spectrum of skin color, there's no way around racism's harms and there's no way around colorism's harms. Colorism at its core is anti-Black. Darker-skinned people suffer directly from the evils of colorism by having fewer opportunities than their lighter-skinned peers, while lighter-skinned folks often feel shunned or judged by those in their community who see their Blackness as less legitimate, less authentic. And so it's important to acknowledge that discussions around colorism will never be easy or simple because, even if by some miracle racism disappeared tomorrow, you cannot erase its legacy from our bloodlines.

Those who've been deemed to be lighter skinned or have

some form of proximity to a white aesthetic can utilize their privilege to effect change and be a major disruptor. A historical figure who epitomizes this is Walter White, who was head of the NAACP for much of the twentieth century. With blond hair and blue eyes, White could have easily passed for white (the play on words here is not intentional, y'all—sorry about that), and in fact did so when providing firsthand accounts of dozens of lynchings and horrifying violence directed against Black citizens of the South. White's reporting was published by the NAACP and became part of the movement to create an antilynching law in America, which was tellingly never enacted. Another political leader who chose Blackness and the Black community over passing was Adam Clayton Powell Jr., a revered Harlem figure and member of the US House of Representatives for two and a half decades. And Diane Nash is yet another Black icon who chose to forgo passing in order to be an invaluable asset to our liberation movement in America.

Reader, for those of you who might have a white-proximate aesthetic, when hearing the anger and pain of those with darker skin who have been subjected to discrimination, I ask for you to listen with an open heart and say, "I very much get it, so let's sit down and unpack this. I'm going to be supportive in whatever way I can." Resist the urge to lean into a "poor light-skinned me" narrative and instead hold space for the reality of our darker kinfolk. And of course, trauma stories aren't the only experiences to be shared here. Many darker-skinned folk have been properly affirmed in their beauty and power. Whatever the case, we can be united in annihilating anti-Blackness. We're in this together.

Fast-forward to my *RHONY* casting and the subsequent related announcements, including the usual marketing campaigns. When I looked at the official Bravo poster announcing Season 13—a diagonal split-screen affair in which we cast members wore shimmering metallic tones in front of a brown background—it was clear to me that I wasn't a big disruption in terms of the general aesthetic the other ladies presented. Some of that just happened naturally, and some of it came about through my own decisions, like choosing to wear my hair straight and at a particular length versus sporting locs or an Afro, for example. There certainly would have been more of an optical disruption to the show if I'd chosen to wear the latter styles. And so I can't help but believe that part of my casting and acceptance, at least on the *RHONY* set, was around me not being too much of an aesthetic deviation from the others. Maybe the hope among producers was that I would simply supplement the cast and that would be that. That I would fit in. After all, how many times do we see shows where the super-cute Black girls, the Lisa Turtles, play second fiddle to the Kelly Kapowskis? (Any *Saved by the Bell* fans out there?) We have been often, at best, the "pretty," popular Black girl who's the sidekick to

to "be the first Black bitch on television." (Remember my advice in the previous chapter about being intentional about how you represent, how to present Blackness in a subversive way?) And when Carroll was cast as Devereaux, when the show's writers were unsure how to write for a Black woman, she simply directed them to craft lines for her character as if she was a white man and she would do the rest. She understood what the realities of her situation were, but by no means felt as if she didn't deserve to be there and occupy space.

So when I thought about how I wanted to show up on *RHONY*, it was that Diahann Carroll–Dominique Deveraux energy I was aiming for. She was often centered in the storytelling, was no one's sidekick, and took up *all* the space whenever she appeared. A divine disruptor extraordinaire.

Even though *RHONY* wasn't aiming to radically rock the boat with my casting—and I looked and dressed the part to blend in—I certainly believed the series knew that it was time to correct years of underrepresentation. Sure enough, when I first walked onto set, I noticed that the crew was *really* white. I was new to reality TV but wasn't new to TV production. One of the first things I always do when I go into set is look for people in production who look like me. When you're making television, when you're telling a story—and that's who we are as media people, storytellers—it's uniquely challenging to tell your tale through the lens of folks who have

BET ON BLACK

an incomplete understanding of your lived experience. Said another way, it's very difficult to effectively tell your story when your colleagues lack cultural competency.

After a few days on set, I made it my business to meet up with a senior-level Black woman producer, a lady who would work on the show throughout my tenure. I was informed that they'd hired a Black woman producer specifically because the network knew that they needed her perspective to effectively produce my story on the show. It was a start, and I took note.

I also went to dinner with Housewife Leah McSweeney a day before we shot our first scene together. We went to the restaurant Nobu with two executive producers and had a natural, unawkward meeting with no stress, no tension. Leah and I were both Virgos and she was converting to Judaism, and I had my own relationship with Black Jewish community building, so there was enough camaraderie there for us to curate, for us to have a working relationship on the show together. Leah had just come off a great Season 12, in which she was a shining star as the only new Housewife. She was young, fresh, a fan favorite, and I think she went into Season 13 feeling as if she would continue that dominance, taking over to mark the new era of *New York*. And I suspect she felt that I would be a great sidekick to that ascension, again regarding me as being a kind of Lisa Turtle to a Kelly Kapowski.

As you can imagine, that was the last damn thing I had in mind. Moving forward, I vowed my work wouldn't revolve around any sidekick bullshit. It would revolve around centeredness and full liberation, not conditional, not subsidiary, but full first-class, American life. D. Deveraux energy full throttle.

BET ON BLACK MOVE

DON'T LET ANYONE MAKE YOU THEIR BLACK SIDEKICK

It's sad to say but the always happy, content Black sidekick is an unfortunate archetype that's lasted for decades on big and small screens alike. This is where our agency and actualization as first-class citizens of the world are given short shrift so the focus can be on the white main character. This mirrors the white power structures of the real world, where Black folks are allowed to be minor players in the field as long as we know our supposed place, as long as we play second fiddle to our white colleagues and associates in schools, workplaces, and other institutions not originally designed for us.

Well, y'all know how I feel about all of that. To hell with that shit. When it comes to how we show up at school or work, be wary of white associates and peers who might seem eager to connect as long as you're centering *their* experiences and desires to achieve as opposed to your own. Pay attention. Take a step back to reflect on the dynamics of your particular situation. Make sure you're clear about what your general objectives are in the workplace, class-room, or any other sort of initiative you're engaging in and that they're front of mind. Now I'm not saying you need to act like a nasty, ruthless bitch and just be about getting yours however you can, but I am saying that you need to center what you wish to gain from a particular work expe-rience in the same way as your white peers. And it's from that place that you should make connections.

Those who can't stand to be around your self-empowerment will slink away like the snakes they are, but those who understand the benefits of mutual help and trust, who don't need to base their self-worth on your subservi-ence and deference, are the ones you should keep close.

The very next day we were shooting at Central Park and I was officially a Housewife. I made sure to wear a Black Lives Matter mask with a long-sleeve hoodie presenting the names of the Central Park Five, aka the five men—Antron McCray, Kevin Richardson, Yusef Salaam, Raymond Santana, Korey Wise—who were wrongfully convicted and imprisoned for years after being coerced by police to admit to a heinous crime that they didn't commit. And that was me being obviously intentional about saying I'm taking up a lot of space before I even open my mouth in terms of cementing my positioning on the show. *Before I open my mouth, y'all got a real Black-ass weapon on the show.* As casual and cool as I played my initial appearance, that was the statement I wanted to make. I hadn't done all this shit, and my ancestors hadn't done what they'd done to survive, for me to take crumbs. No, I wasn't just happy to be there. They were late as fuck and now I was making up for lost time. What folks had to know was that I'd worked my ass off, standing on the shoulders of those who'd come before me, and now I was coming for everything and I wasn't leaving until I got it.

And so my season on *RHONY* progressed from the first Central Park episode to all sorts of reality TV miniscandals and fun, sparkling moments. I won't go into all the permutations of the season, but as I stated in the previous chapter, I was indeed taken to task by a *Vulture* columnist for not understanding the assignment of acting a fool. A few weeks after that write-up came out, a columnist at the *New York Post* wrote an article stating that *RHONY* had gone "woke" and gotten boring because of my presence. Once again, there was a blatant statement that Blackness should be molded to fit the expectations of white audiences, to not see the possibilities that a different perspective could bring.

Okay, for one moment here (and I do mean just for one

moment), I'll set race aside and assert that in addition to my Blackness, I also showed up on *RHONY* presenting a different take on womanhood in general. I showed up as a relatively young, highly educated, professionally astute, sophisticated intellectual. I was a woman with some privilege and some good looks, but I was mostly full of principled substance. That type of woman exists and ought to be represented on *Housewives* at least as much, if not more than, the aloof, ignorant, superficial types.

I was determined to take up space in the way that felt right to me. As I said before, some people said that they felt like in my debut season of *RHONY* that I didn't understand the assignment in terms of what was expected, which was basically C-list shenanigans. But I would counter that argument by asking, just whose assignment are you speaking of? If you're talking about an assignment from some television producers and viewers who feed off of people living in fear and being uncomfortable for the camera, I actually saw that assignment, ripped it up, and threw it in the damn trash. Fuck a fan favorite. My assignment comes from my God on high, and only my God and I know what assignment I should be taking on.

All the things that have made Blackness in America for our forefathers and progeny so horrific and traumatizing and full of pain is rooted in the biggest lie. And now that we know it's a lie, we can name it as a lie, and we can actually decide to take up all the space that we want to, however we want to, given the options available to us. I just decided to take up all the damn space I wanted to on *Housewives*. Nobody gave me permission, and a lot of people to this day are mad about it. I decided this notion of a white-centered space is bullshit, and just as arbitrarily as *RHONY* made the space white centered for thirteen years, I was going to arbitrarily make it Black-centric. As a disruptor, I wasn't even going to negotiate, which was intentional and by design. If y'all had the audacity to center whiteness exclusively even though y'all knew better, I'm coming in hot, full throttle, unapologetically centering my culture and history. And I don't really see the problem there, to make that type of choice in the same way that other choices were made for more than a decade on set and have been for centuries in other spaces.

A lot of my beloved Black folks were mad at me because I was doing some of these things in such an assertive way. Their thoughts were like, *You're going to make these white people so upset that it's making things uncomfortable for the rest of us.* That was the subtext, and what I was communicating was, *I don't negotiate with terrorists.* The consistent subordination of Blackness and the insistence of white centeredness is a form of terrorism, and because I don't negotiate with terrorists, I'm not going to ease myself into certain spaces for the sake of white comfort.

Nonetheless, let me also add that I see no shame in any-one else's game. If another Black woman had opted to take up less *RHONY* space, come in, set her bags down, not touch anything, not say too much, ease her way into the situation, and by her second or third season on the show gradually bring up topics related to Blackness, more power to that sis-ter. And I can understand such an approach considering my time as a broadcaster. I would never indict that methodology. But I also simply refuse to allow anyone to indict mine.

I wanted to unabashedly showcase and celebrate Black beauty, wit, glamour, sophistication, and intellectualism, a departure from the traumatic stories that we've become rou-tinely associated with. That's not to say that we shouldn't be telling, acknowledging, and sitting with very real experiences of Black systemic oppression and injustice and poverty...but that isn't and shouldn't be the only story.

I remember in one of the *RHONY* scenes in Salem, Mas-sachusetts, Housewife Ramona Singer said to me, "You don't look like you've struggled." (Her comment made the news, landing on the *New York Post*'s Page Six.) And I felt disheart-ened that this particular woman had such a powerful tele-vision platform when her only understanding of Blackness was to equate it with trauma and struggle. My entire adult life, different people—Black and white alike—have asked me, "Why so much race talk, Eboni? Why is it always about Blackness?" And my response has always been that in most of the spaces I've occupied, from law to politics to pageantry to reality television, it has been utterly apparent to me that Blackness is the single most misunderstood experience in America. And it was amplified by Ramona's statement.

How is my struggle supposed to look? My retort to Ramona was this: first, the Black American experience isn't only one of struggle; and second, I work particularly hard to make sure I don't always look like a stereotypical story of struggle. That's a disruptive choice I made, even though I don't come from Black affluence. I'm in no way running from the narrative of Black poverty, but these narrowly constructed images and ideas that coincide with Black poverty, and the systemic way in which it those images have been designed, implemented, and reinforced, can be crippling. They end up undermining our right to create a path of physical and spiritual ascension, to create stories for ourselves that more accurately represent who we know ourselves to be. So yes, I was once a poor Black girl, living in subsidized housing, relying on supplemental food stamps utilized by my working mother who eventually decided that my outcomes didn't need to reflect my beginnings.

I will also say, however, that even with the costs of being labeled a *RHONY* disruptor, there've also been profound rewards, particularly the positive feedback I've gotten from some viewers. One weekend, flying back home from a friend's baby shower, an older Black lady who worked at TSA was like, "Girl, you gave it to them. You know, they tried to cut you down, but you gave it to them." And I've heard that often, at sorority conventions and coffee shops and NBA arenas and taxi rides.

About a year ago, after *RHONY*'s season ended, I was once again getting on a plane. And though I was trying to be very undercover in my appearance (code for I looked busted), one of the flight attendants—a six-foot-three, blond-haired, white man—recognized me. "Eboni!" the man exclaimed, and then he almost started tearing up, which took me by surprise.

"Oh my God, you have no idea..." he started to share. "You have no idea know how much I loved you on the last season of *RHONY*, that you actually changed my life." I wasn't quite sure what he meant, but he was such a sweetie pie, promising to take care of me for the duration of the trip. Later on he gave me a handwritten note in which he told me a little bit more about his story. Seeing me stand up for who I was and my culture and community in the face of pushback on the show gave him the strength to actually come out to his family as a gay man.

I teared up, as I was reading Nikole Hannah Jones's *The 1619 Project* book on the flight, and was already deep in my emotions. That moment was so beautiful and powerful to me, showcasing the power of intersectionality. His words were so affirming to what I did on the season regardless of who found it entertaining or not. If the assignment was just to make white people laugh and give them a good time, well, that actually was never *my* assignment. My assignment was to show up as a proud Black woman to represent other Black women and Black people in general, to be gracious, vulnerable, and malleable, but also strong, fiercely educated, determined, and intelligent, creating boundaries around what's acceptable and unacceptable in honoring my humanity. If people like this young man and other people from other communities could see themselves reflected in that positioning of strength in the space that I took up, if those people can fully show up for their own selves and take up more space in their day-to-day lives, and if they can insist on more respect for their humanity, then even better.

My most sincere hope had been realized through my own insistence to show up authentically and wholly. Regardless of who approved of my posture, by centering Blackness I'd inadvertently invited others who found themselves existing outside of the white, hetero, male, Christian norm...to do the same damn thing. I had one statement for all who would listen: "All of us on the margins, you're hereby invited to center yourself...your authentic and complete self in every space you occupy." *That* was my glorious assignment, and anyone who thinks otherwise can take a hike and kiss my Black ass.

I'm extremely proud of how I showed up on Season 13 of *RHONY*, and I gave myself some grace around the fact that it was my first time on a reality show, on a platform of particular pop cultural magnitude. And I think when I rewatch the episodes and see who I was able to be in that space and what it represented to people, I'm going to be like, "All right. That's what I'm talking about."

While I entered *RHONY* full throttle with very clear, overt statements about disruption, my methodology for disruption as a broadcaster was different, more subtle, until the subtlety no longer worked. I'd been working with the NFL Network for about a year and doing stints at the Los Angeles radio station KFI, when one day, in July of 2013, I got an email from a producer at *The O'Reilly Factor* on the Fox News cable channel. Having been at a conservative radio station, I'd heard of the program, of course, which had been around since the mid-1990s, and I knew who Bill O'Reilly was in a cultural context kind of way. But I'd never watched an episode of the show, especially as it appeared on Fox and the network had a reputation. I honestly didn't know enough about who he was or what his platform was all about to be scared or intimidated. The producer had heard me on KFI that morning and wanted to invite me to discuss with O'Reilly and other guests the particularities of one of America's most notorious cases, the acquittal of George Zimmerman. This producer was calling me on the day that a jury in Florida had found Zimmerman not guilty of the second-degree murder of young Trayvon Martin, who was simply walking through a neighborhood when he was deemed to be a "suspicious person" by Zimmerman.

I momentarily grappled with the request. I knew I could go watch an episode of the show and maybe decide, *Oh no, that's not for me, not my vibe.* But I stayed calm and thought things through, and I realized that if anyone needed to hear an astute, clear, nonemotional legal take on what happened in this case—especially from a Black woman—it was the Fox News audience. The principle of disruption was at work here, a principle that would inform my later career choices.

So I agreed to the interview and prepared, choosing to wear my yellow dress, purposely choosing the color as a metaphor that signified I wanted to bring light to the issue. (Yes, I was that literal with my thinking. Don't hate.) I appeared on the New York–based show via video feed from LA. Another analyst, Reverend Jacques DeGraff, appeared live in the studio on the East Coast.

As O'Reilly drilled through the discussion, belligerent and pontificating, I explained that the jury in this case did not find George Zimmerman innocent, and that viewers should not be confused. With the short time I had for the segment, I first discussed why Florida's Stand Your Ground law—which allows those who feel reasonably threatened to use deadly force to defend themselves rather than flee, and which had been a significant part of the discussion of the case—really undermines the legal system as we know it and needs to be eradicated. What this jury found in upholding

Zimmerman's defense of traditional self-defense, and I agree with their findings as a legal scholar, is that the state prosecutor's office, in this case, did not meet their burden of proof. They didn't present enough evidence to prove beyond a reasonable doubt the guilt of this man. What I also didn't get to say because of the segment's time constraints was that I believe the prosecutor also did a poor job of humanizing young Trayvon, not taking into account how Black Americans, especially Black boys and men, have been historically dehumanized. With any murder case, you've got a live defendant who jurors can see touch and almost feel, and you've got an absent victim who is not there in any capacity. So it becomes the prosecutor's job to humanize that individual, in this case that child, to make him real, to make him present so that the jury can project empathy and connection and value onto that individual's life. Again, this is particularly important for Black murder victims.

After my analysis of the case, I got feedback from O'Reilly saying he'd never seen anything like that (his words, not mine), in terms of how I quickly broke down the case. And with the slice of time I had, I was proud of myself. I was able to go on that network and represent myself as someone who was young, Black, beautiful, and highly intellectual. Disruption. I knew many if not most of his viewers didn't generally think about Black people and Black women at that time in this sort of way. I calmly tried to cut through these two grown men, O'Reilly and DeGraff, yelling at each other on live TV. I wasn't flying off the handle, and I wasn't carrying on and screaming. My delivery was the antithesis of their expectations and understanding of Blackness.

I was seen as a big emerging talent at that time. But even with all my success, I was suffering financially. I was working multiple networks, including CNN and HLN, but it wouldn't pay the bills because I wasn't a full-time contributor anywhere. I realized that I was basically appearing as a constant guest, offering my on-air analysis for free. I needed a *real* job, and you know what? The network that made space for me was, surprisingly, Fox News. Yet I'll never sugarcoat my experiences there. After my very first Hannity hit, for instance, my mentions were in shambles as the kids like to say. I had trolls sending in all sorts of comments in response to what I'd said, calling me an Oreo or a raggedy Black bitch or the N word just for asserting the most basic straightforward shit, like, "President Obama's not a terrorist." Despite such nonsense, I managed to do my job.

BET ON BLACK MOVE

ACCESS POWER STRATEGICALLY

When you're in a workplace, especially if you're in a workplace that's predominantly white and thus potentially

hostile to Blackness, it's important to understand the professional terrain. Learn who's in charge, who the key players
are, and research how they got to where they are. Did they
come from money? Are they Ivy Leaguers? Did they pull
themselves up from poverty? How does their background
shape how they operate in professional and public spaces?

I know some folks like to emphasize the warm camaraderie to be found and developed among coworkers. All
good, but I'm sorry, your priority at work shouldn't be primarily about making friends. It's not playtime. You're there
to provide for yourself and your fam, advance your career,
and make demands on behalf of yourself and your community as necessary. Align yourself with the queen/king-
makers who will help you more effectively present your
ideas and fulfill your demands. And as you're aligning, be
mindful of what you offer the dynamic as well. Nobody is
interested in a unilateral relationship. You possess valuable
currency...acute skills, company legacy, and cultural competency, among other assets. Figure out your value and
exchange with the powerbrokers at play in this dynamic.

I was aware of the reality of the situation I found myself
in at Fox, that as much as I used it to advocate for a perspective that would benefit Black folks, I wasn't always going
to be popular with the masses. I would invariably ruffle

feathers, but my perspective and mission for the culture were important.

My approach to the cases I analyzed on-air was intentional and methodical, because I wanted to make it next to impossible for the network to continue to do what they do daily, which was to reduce Blackness and Black Americans to stereotypical tropes and continually dehumanize us by presenting blatant untruths to the masses. My big-picture goal with the network was to represent something that was so obviously other than a stereotype, and subvert the beliefs that could be more easily maintained if I opted to remain out of the spotlight. And this speaks to a piece of advice I'd like to offer to you, dear reader: you don't have to go to work tomorrow, proclaim that you're Black and you're proud, and then blow the whole damn thing up. Disruption can be gradual and strategic, and your path of disruption can take into account where you are in your career, what type of venue you'll be working at, and where you are with *yourself.*

Where I was when I worked for Fox News was different from where I was when I joined the cast of *RHONY*, and my modes of disruption reflected this. When I was on *RHONY*, I felt far freer to disrupt in obvious ways because my professional position was sturdier, my finances were more secure, and I had more credibility. When I was at Fox News, my intention to disrupt had to be gradually expressed because I couldn't come in on day one and be like, *Fuck these white people*. I was going to get me that job, and then, slowly but effectively and strategically over time, get louder and louder in centering Blackness on-air.

But I knew in order to be truly successful with this goal, I would have to eventually have more power at the network. I said it would take five or so years before I got my own show. I went in somewhat gently, never being inauthentic but still being deliberate. Still, over time, what I would share on-air more overtly diverged from what was considered a standard Fox News perspective.

One afternoon, I was guest hosting on the talk show *Outnumbered* with another analyst, a woman named Dagen McDowell. And she was going on and on and on about how President Obama was abusing his power with the number of executive orders he was implementing, that he was a fascist and a disgrace to our country and so on and so forth. And I responded to my cohost that it was her prerogative to like or dislike executive orders, but what we weren't going to do was sit up there and act like Obama had issued the most executive orders of the last three presidents. That title goes to George W. Bush, who issued 291. (Many readers might in fact be shocked to know just how many orders Ronald Reagan issued—381.) I knew this because I always tried to be as prepared as possible for my hosting appearances, and I never said anything on Fox I hadn't previously verified. Plus I'd literally had this debate a year earlier on Gretchen Carlson's show about executive orders and which president had issued the most. But Dagen was going to argue me down on live television, that it was Obama with his unprecedented use of executive orders who was ruining America. And I maintained that, no matter what, if you disliked executive orders under Barack Obama's presidency, you had to concede that you disliked them under George W. Bush. And she wouldn't do it, continuing to imply that somehow Obama's use of executive orders was inherently more nefarious.

We literally went back and forth for about a minute and a half, which is an eternity on live TV. Our argument even got to the point where I had to point out she might be conflating Obama's business regulations with executive orders—completely different things. I straight up asked her if she knew what an executive order was. But I chose to wrap the segment because it became clear to me she was lying or ignorant and I was being positioned as a typical Black Obama defender.

During the commercial break, one of the producers quietly applauded me for holding my ground. The producer also emailed me the actual executive order numbers: Obama, 263 (as of the show date of November 29, 2016), and George W. Bush, 291.

That display of camaraderie highlighted another outlet where I got a little love for what I perceived as acts of disruption. Many of the producers or camera people or other behind-the-scenes staff didn't subscribe to some of the white supremacist thinking that abounded on the network. They were just there for the job, to earn a living. So a lot of times what I would say on-air felt like food for their soul. They were so grateful to have some reasonable, common-sense representation on this stigmatized network where they worked. Everybody that worked there had the stigma that came with Fox, whether you believed the bullshit or not.

On a much more surface level, the Fox women were routinely wearing miniskirts while being all hairsprayed up, which wasn't my forte for obvious reasons. I know what looks good on me, and I made that abundantly clear to producers. No offense, but I didn't let those people touch me for the first year and a half. I wasn't trying to mess with those Mattel crayon colors. I don't play with what I look like on camera, and unless you've demonstrated your ability to improve on what I can do, you will not touch my face. You will not touch my hair, and fuck your wardrobe department. They had a policy that you couldn't wear orange on air, and everybody else had to follow that policy...except me. I knew what looked good on my skin. You might be surprised—or maybe not!—to learn that Fox even had a color wheel for their shows. This is where the executives and the lead host tell you what color you should be wearing to avoid all the women contributors ever wearing the same colors.

I'm not one for stereotyping or making base overgeneralizations, but I do feel comfortable saying that Black people often have a knack for displaying exquisite style, especially Black women, who are typically the fashion queens of whatever space we occupy, whatever street we walk down, establishing trends around the world. Badass. I mean, it's only because of structural racism that it took so long for someone like Rihanna to have her own fashion house.

Many of us have an understanding of what adornment and grand presentation can do for our individual spirits and the tenor of the world. At the same time, when entering spaces that weren't designed for us, you might encounter subtle or overt messaging about your appearance. The messaging might imply that a specific Black aesthetic normally seen as beautiful in our communities is making the powers that be uncomfortable. We've seen the controversies that have erupted over Black folks who have worn braids or other types of natural hairstyles, such as journalist Melissa Harris-Perry; in fact, over the years scores and scores of Black people have been fired from their jobs for showing up with hairstyles that were deemed inappropriate for the workplace. Cue the Crown Act.

I would assert that anyone who challenges your rights to your own beautiful Black body must simply have to get over it. This is just another form of Black subordination and the centering of Eurocentric style. Once again, be strategic, making sure that workplace guidelines are fulfilled, especially as the latter could be considered a form of discrimination. Also be sure to point out to a manager how Black people have historically and unfairly faced pushback from employers over our appearance.

Alas, matters of appearance and an authentic Black aesthetic would become the least of my worries the longer I stayed on the troubled network. In April 2017, just months before the #MeToo movement took off, Bill O'Reilly got canned after being confronted with a new series of sexual harassment allegations. This was not long after Roger Ailes had been removed as chairman of Fox News over sexual harassment allegations as well. It was fucking crazy town and even more disgusting and revealing than I was unfortunately used to, and like any other corporate worker trying to pay her bills, I tried to stay focused, as amid all of that, I was navigating a promotion for a permanent hosting position. That would mean my own show, my own terms. Everybody in the building thought I was going to get a permanent job there. I didn't. And that's when I realized it was time to leave the network. We saw this with *Today*'s Tamron Hall and NBC, with the network offering Fox's Megyn Kelly her own multimillion-dollar-contract show (which would ultimately be canceled after only a year because the foolish woman defended acts of blackface) over their own sparkling, highly qualified talent who was a person of color. And so Tamron left. When you keep getting passed over for a role that's rightfully yours, that's the indication that there's no more room for you to ascend in that particular professional space. And you must, for your own sake, bet on Black and move on.

There were some other ups and then disappointing downs in between the rest of what I'm going to share that ultimately caused me to hand in my metaphorical resignation card, *boop, done, y'all*, but what led me to really do it was ultimately this...

Charlottesville happened, and I really had to wake the fuck up.

On August 12, 2017, hundreds of people descended into Charlottesville, Virginia, to participate in what they called the Unite the Right rally. The group consisted of armed white supremacists who let their anti-Blackness, anti-brownness, and anti-Semitism be widely known via their chants and gestures, with the ostensible goal of saving Lee Park, with its statue of Robert E. Lee, from being renamed. The Unite the Right participants were met by counterprotesters that morning, and violence ensued, with the governor declaring a state of emergency. A thirty-two-year-old counterprotester, Heather Danielle Heyer, was killed after being struck by a car driven by a white supremacist who bored into the crowd, injuring nineteen other people. And two police officers, Berke M. M. Bates and H. Jay Cullen, were killed when their helicopter crashed as they attempted to deal with the conflict.

The then president of the United States, Donald Trump, eventually issued a statement at a news conference where he asserted that though there were bad folks among the Unite the Right rally participants, there were also "very fine people on both sides." Which means that yes, the president of the most powerful country in the world was stating that there were nice, fine people among white supremacists who uttered slogans like "Jews will not replace us," whose set of beliefs facilitated one of their own murdering a brave young ally who believed in equality and inclusivity so much that she took her beliefs to the street.

As I saw all that had occurred, I had to decide who I was going to be in this moment, because now it was a do-or-die situation. If I said what really needed to be said in this moment, my career as I knew it at Fox News was done. It was over. But if I didn't speak the truth, then I could only ask myself, *Bitch, why are you here?* How was I going to live with myself if I didn't honestly address this day in American history? If something like the Unite the Right rally happens on my watch and I don't say what needs to be said as a Black-conscious woman in America, I'm a piece of shit. That was my analysis. I'm a piece of shit on everything, and I would only prove the haters right who'd said that I was a self-serving hypocrite of Black consciousness by being on Fox in the first place.

I decided to honor my positioning and say exactly what

needed to be said. On August 14, 2017, I presented my on-air docket, responding to President Trump's statements regarding the violence in Charlottesville with these words:

Mr. President, your initial remarks were cowardly and dangerous, and they indeed warranted a second statement. Here's why: your presidential campaign slogan—"Make America great again"—well, it [raised] many questions for many. Are Jews, Blacks, gays, and Hispanics included in America's return to her great glory years, or would some of us be left out? I was legitimately unsure. But absent more conclusive evidence, I was willing to give you the benefit of the doubt. I can no longer do that, Mr. President. No more benefit, all doubt. In a moment where you could've been crystal clear where you stand on the issue of inclusion, standing up against white supremacy and domestic terrorism, you very intentionally chose to be ambiguous, to equivocate. "All sides," Mr. President? Please.

President Trump, I do not know your heart, but what I do know for sure is that you've clearly done the math, and you've decided that your portion of the base that is absolutely racist is so significant, so valuable, that you hesitate, even in the face of blatant, flagrant hatred, to risk turning them off and thereby crippling your political stronghold...While you personally may not be a racist, President Trump, what you are is all too happy to reap the benefits of their support, and you even tacitly encourage them with evasive, irresponsible statements.

And so it went.

My docket made national news and went viral, also garnering national and international coverage from mainstream news outlets while ending my TV news career in general. I'd made news for being the Fox host who refused to go along with the corporate group message.

As I was writing my docket, I'd made peace with everything that would come after that. You couldn't be a host on a Fox News show and make the kind of comments I'd made to that audience and expect to continue as if everything was hunky-dory. The solo show would never happen and I probably wouldn't be renewed after my contract was up in another year and a half. They still had to continue to give me some on-air time, and I now felt liberated to do whatever the hell I wanted to do, which in this network's case was to call total and complete bullshit every time I saw it or got close to it. My notion of disruption had entered a new phase.

Meanwhile, I was nuclear at the time. Audiences hated me to the point where I was getting death threats and I had to have security escort me. It was that bad, and security was pulled after only two weeks. I was scared. I was scared of being recognized on the street, because if you're a fanatical

Trump person and you feel like I'm a threat to your positioning, there's not a lot you won't do to protect that positioning, as we saw on January 6. So those were the stakes for me,
and they were very real.

I was sent to Washington, DC, to cover regular news
for an anchor who would be on maternity leave. But after
I confronted future governor of Georgia Brian Kemp about
his overt voter suppression tactics, I was pulled off of doing
full newscasts. Execs thought if I kept on confronting guests
that I was going to get myself killed, no one was going to
watch anything I was on, or people were going to start boy-
cotting the network.

By December of 2018, I asked to be let out of my contract
slightly early, and other opportunities were brewing. But I'd
made it clear to millions of viewers what it meant to be a
Black professional who, when push came to shove, unequivocally aligned herself with shove.

And this goes back to what I'd explained at the beginning
of this chapter, that there's a cost to making demands, that
there's a cost to being a disruptor if this is the path you
(hopefully) choose. You're not fucking shit up just to fuck
shit up. You're doing it to have a breakthrough, to reshape
spaces. I know that it's easy to say to go ahead and be a disruptor, to go blaze a trail on behalf of your people. But what
do you do when you get the call that your disruption is making people uncomfortable, that they want you to stop...or

else? It's a risk, so you need to brace yourself against losing money, opportunity, and status. Being a disruptor cost me a job and, temporarily, a sense of well-being even though I'd always operated from a place of truth and principle. And then my time on *RHONY* cost me my popularity. But the *RHONY* experience also affirmed my instincts. Douglass has told us that power concedes nothing without a demand. Be clear about your demand and be equally clear about what you're willing to give up for that demand, because avenues of power will demand your sacrifice. They always have and always will.

To be honest, my time on *RHONY* eventually went past disruption and became an active protest. And because of my chosen form of protest—to center Blackness on a show that had twelve years of being white-centric in one of the most diverse metropolises in the world—I paid the price. I was fired, making me the most infamous and impactful one-season Housewife in Bravo history. Yet I was happy to be fired if my firing created a path forward for a better, more inclusive, more accurate *RHONY*, and a better American society. I'm proud of my actions, and they were worth the cost.

What has gotten me through it all is my unwavering faith in God. During tough moments, my darkest days in our fight, I listen to the words of Dr. Martin Luther King Jr. "But If Not" is a sermon delivered by Dr. King in 1967 at Ebenezer Baptist Church in Atlanta, Georgia. He speaks powerfully and simply about the difference between an "if faith" and a "though faith."

The "if faith" says that if all goes well for me, if I'm prosperous and I don't get called bad names for taking a stand that I feel I must take, if none of these things happen, then I'll pay my tithes, show up on Sunday, and have faith in God. But the "though faith" says, though things go wrong, though I'm condemned and persecuted, nevertheless I'm gonna believe in God anyway. The "if faith" is contingent on the comforts of life while the "though faith" is the permanent everlasting faith.

As the sermon concludes, Dr. King suggests that somewhere along the way we each discover some principle or some issue so dear, so eternally worthy that we'll never give it up. Something that we'll never negotiate. Thus we can say, "I know my God will deliver me, *but if not*, I'm going on anyway and I'm going to stand up for what I believe in anyway." He goes on to say that in the final analysis, you do right not to avoid a hellacious existence, but you do right because it's *right* to do right. You do right because your guiding principle has gripped you so much that you're willing to die for it if necessary. Dr. King asserts that if you haven't found something so dear to you that you'd die for it, then you aren't fit to live.

Dr. King says you might be thirty-eight years old (as he happened to be while delivering his remarks) and an opportunity stands before you, calling upon you to stand up for some great issue, some great cause. And you refuse to do so because you're afraid that you'll lose your job or social status and be criticized. You could go on to live until you're ninety, but you're just as dead at thirty-eight as you would be as an elderly person because you died the moment you refused to stand up for truth and justice. The good reverend coined this a "double death." And I for one am not interested in a premature death. I've got too much to do and too much to live for.

When Dr. King spoke about "double death," I hear him saying that when you finally realize what you were born to do, you *must* act on that purpose. I know exactly why I was put on this earth. I was born as a further proof of concept for my community, proof that whiteness doesn't have a stronghold on intelligence, beauty, femininity, sophistication, ambition, and accomplishment. And proof that even with the associated costs of protest and disruption, we as Black people will continue to find pathways to a blissfully uncompromising mode of divine humanity.

CHAPTER 4

COUNSEL

"As iron sharpens iron, so one person sharpens another."

—PROVERBS 27:17

ALL RIGHT, Y'ALL, SO MUCH OF this book so far has been focusing on how we can actualize our Blackness as individuals, about the ways in which we can center our history and perspectives in order to have a first-class, fully liberated experience in America. But I'm going to shift now to the importance of a beloved community, a phrase Dr. King famously used. I'm going to shift to the spiritual and political importance of being interconnected with others, of helping each other out when we're faced with life's inevitable challenges as Black folk. A fundamental aspect of Blackness is for us to be in continual community with each other, and that for us to operate in isolation from others is essentially anti-Black. And I'm here to proclaim, as part of the good news of Blackness, that we no longer need to operate from a place of separation, that we can strategically choose to surround ourselves with various forms of support as part of a fully liberated Black experience in America.

James Baldwin also wrote about this need to be with community when he made the decision to return to America after having lived in France for several years. For all intents and purposes, Baldwin could have stayed in Europe permanently and continued to write there, but he maintained that he needed to be back among Black people.

An essential strategy in our enslavers' efforts to dehumanize us was to destroy our sense of community with each other. Enslavers would send away mothers and fathers and children and friends to be sold off to other plantations and properties, with their loved ones having no way to trace where they were taken. The trauma of such efforts has affected us for generations. As a consequence, according to Professor Rheeda Walker, director of the University of Houston's Culture, Risk, and Resilience Lab, for so many Black people "'getting help' is seen as a weakness, so folks press on even when they are struggling. Doing so is part of a cultural legacy of survival in the face of brutal circumstances." Our heritage of survival under white supremacy has damaged our ability to be in community with each other in powerful, life-saving ways.

I grieved openly when my friend Cheslie Kryst took her life. Cheslie was an attorney and an athlete with an MBA degree. She was also a pageant queen who won the Miss USA crown in 2019, at the age of twenty-eight becoming the oldest contestant to earn the title. She was cognizant of what her win meant for the larger community, as she wrote in a 2021 article for *Allure* magazine: "Pageant girls are supposed to be model-tall and slender, don bouffant hair, and have a killer walk. But my five-foot-six frame won with six-pack abs, earned after years of competing in Division I Track and Field, and a head of natural curls in a time when generations of Black women have been taught that being 'too Black' would cost them wins in the boardroom and on pageant stages."

Cheslie was fiercely vocal about her activism work and belief in the power of her Blackness, letting her perspective inform her work as a correspondent for the entertainment news show *Extra*. This sister was so good at what she did that she earned two Daytime Emmy nominations as part of the *Extra* team.

But Cheslie also wrote in that *Allure* article about feeling like she was constantly chasing achievements to the point of undermining her physical health and emotional well-being. She found herself wondering about the point of all her achievements if she wasn't properly enjoying her life. Chelsie was a beautiful soul, and I was honored to call her a friend. Having been raised in North Carolina like yours truly, Cheslie was a proud Black woman of biracial ancestry who chose to center her life in her Blackness. But when she plummeted to her death from her high-rise New York apartment in what was officially ruled a suicide, shocking so many of us in her life personally and those who were fans around the nation, I spent nights thinking about the isolation she must have felt and what she stated in the *Allure* article that might've been overlooked because of her very public success and the environment of friends and family who loved her. I'm not aware of what demons Cheslie might have been contending with in her inner world, but I do know that she gave so much of herself to the public and that she regularly showed up in community with those of us who appreciated all that she could do.

What I understand from Cheslie's article and from being Black in America is that there is a constant feeling of isolation and separation that we have endured since the days of slavery. It has simply become part of our survival. It takes a village to ensure that we survive and thrive, but many Black people will tell you how they've also had to push through many difficult moments alone, with limited support to help get them where they are. This survival instinct, along with our ability to rise up and conquer shit even in the toughest circumstances, is what makes us unique as a culture. It makes us special as individuals, and the good news is, as a people and a community, it makes us invincible when we get together.

But there's a catch-22 here. The unintended cost of our resilience and ability to push through challenges is that we're sometimes not taking sufficient care of our spirit. We're sometimes not taking time to really sit with what we need to be healthy, listening to that inner voice or higher power that maybe says we need to take a break from pushing and just be still, or maybe not be so tough and brave. That maybe it's time to be soft and fluid and lean on those who care for us.

Most of us make it through tough spots with the support and kindness of our community in one way or another. And I'm openly acknowledging this here and now because we need to abandon this notion of being perennially tough, high-achieving Black individuals who can do shit on our own. White people love to give the example of Barack Obama as an all-time paragon of Black success who pulled himself up by his bootstraps to soaring heights of greatness, as if this is the best way to become somebody. In reality, this description of his rise is a myth. There were all kinds of people who supported Obama and helped him achieve his success, especially Black people. The Obama myth connects to this notion that we can only be successful as long as we bear society's challenges individually and keep it moving. Absolutely not. It's just another trifling example of how larger society gets Blackness all wrong, denying us the full range of our experiences as human beings. Part of Blackness is to make ourselves vulnerable, to allow ourselves to be supported and taken care of, to laugh, to play, to have experiences of life that have nothing to do with pushing toward something.

The cost of this feeling of isolation that we're sometimes left with is severe, especially when we feel like we're alone in our need and fight for equity. Or when we feel stressed with the load that's involved in providing for ourselves and our families in an economically tough America that was ravaged by a pandemic.

According to the American Psychiatric Association, even though Black Americans suffer from mental illness at similar rates to other populations in the US, we tend to have much less access to mental health services. Thus only a *third* of Black folks who need professional intervention actually receive it. This lack of access contributed to the increasing rate of suicide we saw among Black folks prior to the appearance of COVID-19, a disturbing trend that has only continued during the pandemic. According to the US Department of Health and Human Services, suicide has become the second leading cause of death among Black Americans aged fifteen to twenty-four. And in California, the most populous state in America, with almost forty million people, there's been a skyrocketing suicide rate among Black people aged eighteen to twenty-four.

Taking time for community is an essential part of our

experience and well-being that has been overlooked. Taking time for connectedness is an essential part of our experience, in the same way that knowing our history or subverting racist representation is. As a community, we're pushing back on Black narratives that seem intent on centering our suffering, that emphasize our trauma over our layered humanity and beauty. Instead, we're embracing our care. Champion athletes like Naomi Osaka and Simone Biles made it their business to step back from their sports for their own self-care, and we backed them up on that. We supported what they needed and not what white supremacy has taught us about what Black women and athletes need to be, the Black champion who pushes through all the bullshit. Nope. The Black community isn't taking any of it anymore.

The Black community and this sense of being a part of a collective is often how we get the best shit done and take care of each other. If you're struggling or need help or support with something, I challenge you to reach out to your community for access and solutions. There'll be something for you, I guarantee it. (And I've also provided some resources highlighting Black care at the end of the book.) We wouldn't have survived and created such an astounding legacy without what we do for each other.

My primary way of accessing support is in the form of what I call my personal board of directors. I had to somehow acknowledge that my friends, AKA sorors, and my family members may come from different sectors of my life but still have a cohesive purpose—and frankly, a seriousness of purpose—that I'm grateful for. These are the people I innately trust to help deal with conflicts and challenges. They're pivotal in helping me grapple with my biggest life decisions, in helping to steer my ship, so to speak, toward safe harbors. That's what a board of directors does with whatever organization they're entrusted to oversee. And my members are about five individuals who provide invaluable assistance and counsel to me. I believe in my professionalism, intelligence, decision-making skills, and so on, but nobody has a 360-degree perspective when it comes to their life. And the comprehensive perspective from my personal board is important. Of course, not everyone on your board needs to be Black, but you do need to include people who identify with you as a Black person—and that's usually a fellow Black person. And so I would say that's a key thing to do when selecting your personal board of directors in general, to make sure to examine the ways in which your team can have your back in complementary ways.

One member of my board is a nonprofit executive who specializes in the financial sphere. Another member is a queer man who's an intellectual giant, serving as the executive director of a massive nonprofit after having earned his doctorate. And another is a former on-air talent who transitioned to owning her own business and a talent agency, while another is a high-level network exec who used to be my boss at a previous gig. My lawyer, in fact, is on my personal board. Sometimes our conversations are about the nature of our legal dealings while other times they're about broader life decisions. So it's really nice to have the duality of that relationship there—from someone who also happens to be a former mentee from law school—a full-circle experience.

Here's an example of how my board was quite invaluable during one of the most difficult periods of my life—the dissolution of my engagement to my former fiancé. This was a relationship that I'd been in for almost four years during my midthirties, a relationship that I deemed the most significant of my adult life. I was partnered with the man I thought I would spend the rest of my days with. So much of what I've talked about in this book—starting from the Fox News of it all to the *RHONY* of it all to *REVOLT Black News*—all of that stuff happened while I was in this relationship. And my fiancé was such a bedrock of support. But by 2020, I started to take an honest assessment of my life, looking at what was working and what wasn't working, and what I wanted the next chapter to look like. I realized that I was emotionally tethered to this individual and the history we'd created as a couple. But something felt off. There were no massive red flags or unacceptable modes of behavior. There was no infidelity or abuse or any kind of emotional or physical violence. But I just knew instinctively something felt off,

bend themselves enough to where such a setup would certainly have a cost but could still actually work. But she and I had known each other for over twenty years, and she knew I wasn't flexible in that way. "If you further concede what you want out of this life for the sake of this relationship, you will not be you anymore," she said. "You won't just be compromising over smaller things; you'll be compromising yourself." And she knew that was unacceptable to me, that it just wasn't possible for me to live that way.

This friend's approach was relatively direct while other people were better at listening and asking pointed, thoughtful questions. Another member of the board knew that if he asked the right set of consecutive questions, it would lead me to my own conclusion. And then there was another friend who played devil's advocate around the whole thing. The vibe was like, "Let's play this out. Let's say you guys actually do get married and do this. What's that calculation like for you? How close is that to what you actually want versus what you would lose by compromising?" She challenged me to play out scenarios, even including potential choices that she didn't think would be right. But she still thought it was important to talk things out and see where we landed, and then make evaluations based around that potential choice. As an attorney, as someone who values the Socratic method, this approach was invaluable.

And frankly, all of my friends' approaches were invaluable,

illuminating why having a board of distinct individuals is essential to making good decisions. These folks can help you see things that may not be immediately clear from just one or two POVs. Is there something that you've been struggling with for a while, where a range of honest feedback seems to be in order? When it came to making a decision about my relationship, I needed a certain amount of variety suffused with kindness. Imagine if everybody on the board had been like, "Bitch, you're just stupid! Get out of that thing with that man. Y'all obviously don't work, so why are we even talking about this?" Well, I suspect I would've had a pretty defensive reaction to the advice and been shut down emotionally. Instead, I needed some sweet sauce and some hot sauce, some tenderness and tough love, and that's exactly what I got.

And I'm spelling this out for y'all in such detail because I want it to be super clear how you can create these structures for yourself to enable your survival, growth, and evolution. Be mindful of your weaknesses, of the ways in which your board can supplement something that you may lack, and—vice versa—you can think of ways you can be of service to individual members of your board as well. And let's be clear: the issues that come up for you may not directly involve issues around race or racialized trauma. I certainly don't envision Black lives being primarily defined by the racism we experience. And you can have people on your board who aren't Black. I would nevertheless maintain that you need to make sure you're comfortable centering your Blackness when you connect with your board about your experiences, and whether your board is fully or partially Black, that they're wholly comfortable with this. We have been asked for too long to keep our Blackness out of leading narratives, and we're simply not doing this anymore. As proud Black people, our Blackness will be a part of any conversation that we feel it should be. If anyone on your board isn't comfortable with this, if you receive any sort of direct or indirect passive-aggressive pushback from someone for seeing the world through the lens of Blackness and our history, then they're not a particularly valuable board member and you should kick their ass to the curb.

BET ON BLACK MOVE

WITH YOUR PERSONAL BOARD, BE CHOOSY

Please be sure to be choosy with whom you select for your board, with whom you turn to for advice in your hours of need. If you know someone who's addicted to weed, smacks around his girlfriend, lies to his parents, and always has to borrow money to pay rent—this is obviously *not* someone to add to your board. Look at people who are generally happy, who occupy places in life that genuinely speak to their interests, who exhibit baseline decency to themselves and other people. You don't need to agree with everything that they do or say, you don't need to have the same political beliefs or religious beliefs, but you do need to respect how these people walk their walk on this planet.

I know firsthand the power of being in community with people who have your back professionally as well, where your Blackness can be fully expressed and celebrated. Those stressful, final days with Fox epitomized to me what could happen if you moved too far away from home and the people you know to be your community. My habit of achieving my way out of personal trauma just wasn't working anymore. After the circumstances of my tenure there, I suffered from depression and almost crippling bouts of anxiety. And I only got through all of this by establishing new professional networks that spoke to my Blackness.

I was losing credibility in my own community fucking around with Fox, and thus I needed to rehabilitate my reputation, something that was supremely important to me.

It had gotten to the point where a fellow journalist who will remain nameless had taken me to task via social media for a misspelling appearing on a caption that appeared underneath my face as I was giving a report, as if I was responsible for writing the captions.

Most Black people weren't watching the station, so they

didn't know that I actually had our backs while lighting up certain commentators. They thought that the association I'd created with the network immediately implied that I wholeheartedly supported its politics, and that I was unforgivably whack for doing so.

One day, weeks after I'd decided to leave Fox, it dawned on me that if I needed to let my people know what I was doing on behalf of myself and the culture, I had to go deliver that message directly. I wanted to get on the radio show *The Breakfast Club*.

I'd already worked in radio before, so I knew I would be extremely comfortable with the format and I'd be able to connect with my community on a platform where they were respected and felt engaged. I would occasionally see *Breakfast Club* host Charlamagne tha God in the Fox News green room when he made appearances on the show *KennedyNation*, hosted by former MTV VJ Kennedy. I would light up every time I saw him. In fact, anytime I saw Black folks in the building, I felt like it was a holiday. (I know my corporate readers can relate.) One day I told Charlamagne about my epiphany, letting him know I would love to come on his show and talk to his audience about my work and background. My plan was to do an amazing job and then broach the subject about being a host on the show. It was all working out when he said, "Great. Yeah, here's my email. Be sure to reach out." But even though this green room exchange happened two or three times, he never responded when I did send an email.

After time spent campaigning for a slot, I finally got booked, appearing with Charlamagne as well as cohosts Angela Yee and DJ Envy. Overall the appearance went great, and I was able to speak openly about who I am and my general politics while sharing some unadulterated truths about my career. I also gently expressed to Charlamagne that I was slightly hurt that he had availed himself of the opportunity to appear on Kennedy's show but hadn't reciprocated by offering that level of visibility to a Black woman at the network who wanted to appear on his show. Cohost Angela graciously showed her support for me as a fellow woman of color. And Charlamagne sat there calmly and listened as we unpacked it all like grown folks. This started a fantastic relationship between Charlamagne and me that is very much rooted in candor and mutual respect.

And wow, was I happy as a guest on *The Breakfast Club*. In just a few appearances on the show, I felt more supported and appreciated than I ever had in all my previous years as a broadcast journalist. At *The Breakfast Club*, I didn't have to choose between utilizing pristine, King's English when I spoke and deploying a profane four-letter word at just the right moment, something that would've been fucking unthinkable when I was working as a journalist on CBS or Fox. I got to use both modes of language, which I enjoy, and with no unspoken assumption that I would tiptoe around truth with some bullshit. I didn't have to choose between being comfy in Walker Wear sweats (shout-out to designer April Walker, queen of urban streetwear!) and sporting my sexy Christian Louboutin pumps. Again, I could do both, with no inane, oppressive color wheel put in place by people who were clueless when it came to celebrating Black style. I was able to show up in a way where I could breathe while sharing knowledge that I hoped viewers and listeners would appreciate. I realized that with each *Breakfast Club* appearance I increasingly got to be my most authentic, unadulterated self. It was something that became essential to my emotional and mental survival. It wasn't until I'd developed my podcast *Holding Court* that I experienced that same level of liberation and freedom. Appearing on *The Breakfast Club* and engaging with my community, it was like, finally, after years of being out in the wilderness with little food and barely any water, my ass had finally come on home, and my spirit soared.

Up until that time, there had been very few places where I got to exist as a creative, showing up aesthetically and rhetorically in such full capacity. I have deep appreciation for that feeling of safety, and it affirmed what I've always known about Blackness and our people, that we can support different types of experiences in the spaces we create. I appreciate that my people made space for me to show up in my full intensity and honor my Black experience. And that's probably why the very best content that I'd ever produced thus far showed up on that platform. My spirit felt like it could soar, like maybe it was safe to sing a little song and do a little strut.

And most important, I no longer felt the need to code switch as I'd done at previous media outlets, where I'd adopted modes of language and style that fit narrow, white notions of professionalism. I could be freely me. And that's what I want for all of my readers: to know that code switching should be a thing of the past, that we have every right to show up in professional spaces with our distinctive language, style, and modes of thought.

As we discussed with the board of directors and community, once we take a closer look at what people are doing with their time and power, we can get a better sense of how we want to show up and what we want to do. This is what betting on the Black community will do for you personally. It's important to note that each of *The Breakfast Club*'s hosts inspired how I viewed what I could do with my work and influence. (Hence, projects like this book—Sis has things she needs to say out loud for us! This book gives me the platform to proclaim these things and have these perspectives passed down within our community, not depending on others to do so for me. And through this book, conversations among us can be created that can blossom into expansion and productivity for our people.) Charlamagne's someone who's constantly curious, quick to acknowledge exactly what he knows and doesn't know. But what he is able to do, he does brilliantly. And I think that's why he's so important to Black and brown culture. He recognizes the impact of his platform and understands the value of his reach. When he touches something or amplifies someone, it just hits differently. And so does his ability to exert his influence on the culture and make calculations and use his own spiritual discernment to determine what he thinks the culture needs more of— whether that's education about homeownership, mental health conversations...whatever it is, it just hits differently. He's a courier of currency to the culture.

Angela Yee is a constant support sister and unflinchingly has my back and others', after carving out a space for herself in what can be a hostile media environment for Black women. She's a full-on business mogul, having several properties, including a juice bar in Brooklyn, and curating a dominant real estate portfolio. She's someone I look up to, and I aspire to duplicate what she's been able to accomplish in terms of wealth building while providing a health-oriented service for Black people and brown people. She has a vision for herself and our community beyond being a host on a leading show, and she shows us that these achievements can be manifested both one individual at a time and as a collective.

The first couple of times I went on the show, I was honestly very intimidated to interact with DJ Envy. He was the shiny bright thing of the program, the one who had earned all sorts of accolades over the years due to his mixtape work and collaborations with a bevy of stars that included Jay-Z, Cam'ron, and Janet Jackson. I made assumptions about what he would be like. And then somebody told me in a preproduction call on REVOLT TV that Envy's father used to be a sergeant, and I said, "Get out of here." Now I see him as Sean, the son of a Black cop in New York who became a husband, father, and icon in the culture who has his own deep, personal relationship with what it is to be a Black man in relationship with law enforcement. Each of these hosts has taught me something major about how expansive I can be.

Allowing yourself to be vulnerable with others in the Black community can be a terrifying thing, this I know, but supporting each other has always been essential to our community's survival during the harshest of times. And, during my midnight hour, *The Breakfast Club* trio had my back.

It is not always an easy thing, to ask others for help and honest feedback, to hear so many things that you may not want to hear, I get it. But the growth you'll experience if you do so is invaluable. It can be a literal lifesaver. Regardless of whether you choose to create a personal board or not, you need to know that support is all around us. We simply have to make the decision to accept it, to let this support change us, and when the time comes, allow ourselves to be in community with others.

CHAPTER 5
ENTITLED

"It is a peculiar sensation, this double-consciousness, this sense of always looking at one's self through the eyes of others, of measuring one's soul by the tape of a world that looks on in amused contempt and pity. One ever feels his two-ness—an American, a Negro; two souls, two thoughts, two unreconciled strivings; two warring ideals in one dark body, whose dogged strength alone keeps it from being torn asunder."

—W. E. B. Du Bois,
The Souls of Black Folk

need to distance ourselves from the country that is ours, a country deeply informed by Blackness in myriad ways. Quite simply, America doesn't realize how Black it is, how over the centuries Black labor, spirituality, intellectualism, and culture have created the country that so much of the world has come to celebrate. When it comes to our labor, from the time of ancestral enslavement to when we joined the workforce as legally emancipated people, we built this nation on our backs, and we have as much right to claim it as our counterparts, if not more so.

Black creative output is probably the most obvious thing to jump into when it comes to looking at how we've shaped the country, as there are a plethora of examples of how we've profoundly impacted everything from the arts to fashion to sports. Calling out our impact on music is a no-brainer, with the American sonic landscape composed almost entirely of songs that can trace their origins to Black communities. Yes, I know it might be hard for some white folks to fathom, but even the whitest, most grunge-tinged hard rock bands out there wouldn't exist without rock and roll pioneers like Fats Domino, Little Richard, and Chuck Berry. The slick R&B music of today that's coveted by the world has its roots in traditional blues, jazz, and soul. Decades ago, it would've been unheard of for hip-hop, created by Black and Latinx communities in the Bronx, to be a major contender on the music charts or traditional awards shows like the Grammys, but now hip-hop routinely dominates the world of music, to the point where rock—which was once such a pop music mainstay for white listeners—is practically nowhere to be found. Turning to fashion, it's now standard for couture runways to feature styles informed by streetwear sensibilities, with "streetwear" basically being a term used to sum up what young, urban Black and Latinx folks are wearing. And do I really need to go into the multitude of ways in which Black vernacular ("diss" ... "jive" ... "jiggy" ... "bad" ... "around the way" ... "dolla" ... "boogie" ... "bootie" . . . "thottie" ... "get down" ... and the list goes on) has been incorporated into the American lexicon throughout generations?

I mean, I could be here all damn day providing examples of magnificent Black cultural output and still not be done by the time night rolled around. And our nation can't have it both ways. America can't co-opt the culture we created for consumption by the masses while expecting us to be content with second-class status, relinquishing the wealth, privileges, and birthright that white people have accessed for generations. We have every right to proclaim our Americanness, to let others know that the country would be a shell of what it is without all that we and our ancestors have contributed.

I understand this reluctance that many in our community have around standing up and saying "I'm proud to be an American" considering the history of this country, where we've endured hundreds of years of enslavement and second-class citizenship via laws and social practices. There's a part of us that's sitting with the question, "If I fully adopt an American identity, does it mean that I'm asking to be white, that I'm somehow embracing white supremacy?" I say without hesitation, "No, of course not." But again, I understand the ambivalence that comes up, as there's been such a gross distortion over the years of what being American means. It feels like the word "America" has really meant "white" for as long as I can remember, with every other ethnic or racial group that resides here needing to be hyphenated to claim American bona fides. For Black folks, these distortions have ended up defining our relationship to our country, taking away our right to decide freely for ourselves what this relationship should be.

Black self-perception has been impacted by American racism for generations, which is why I started this chapter with a quote from our scholar-prince W. E. B. Du Bois. The leading intellectual of the Black community for much of the twentieth century, Du Bois published his landmark work *The Souls of Black Folk* in 1903. The book contains the essay "Of Our Spiritual Strivings," and in it Du Bois wrote of this concept of Black people developing a double consciousness. This was a mind-set where, post-slavery, we dealt both with the realities of our lives as Black people while also navigating a white world where our concerns were positioned as secondary, if they were even thought about at all. And thus we've had to create two separate modes of consciousness to survive these terrible circumstances and maintain our society. This double consciousness has often meant that we feel like we need to fully divorce ourselves from general American life in order to claim our authentic Blackness.

Fast-forward decades later from the time Du Bois offered these words, after the civil rights movement. The distortions that emanate from having a double consciousness are still a significant part of the Black experience. As a child, I received all sorts of ideas about this concept of national identity for Black people that weren't particularly helpful. I gradually got the message from the media and from watching adults that if you were a nice, respectable Black who played by the rules as dictated by white people, if you never protested or complained, then perhaps you could one day claim Americanness, even though you would probably never be considered a true American by many in the larger society.

On the other hand, if you were a radical rabble-rouser who actively prioritized the elevation of Black life and consciousness whenever you could, then you forfeited your right to be considered a real American by practically everyone. It was all about keeping your yap shut, or else.

Our nation has also aggressively denied Black Americans the chance to forthrightly claim a sense of patriotism. When I was in high school, I was horrified to learn that when Black soldiers returned home from World War I, many of them were murdered, lynched, and attacked simply for returning to their homeland with their military uniforms on. Why? Because the optics of a Black man with a United States military uniform on made too audacious of a statement of American belongingness. Even after giving our lives in every American war and political conflict since the American Revolution, the hostile denial of Black Americans' right to full patriotism persists.

As stated, sometimes we Black folks understandably concede our patriotism in knowing ways, purposely choosing to distance ourselves from the American project after all the years of racism we have endured, while other times the concession is unconscious. Nikole Hannah Jones opens the first episode of her *1619* podcast with a story about her Black American father proudly displaying the American flag on their front lawn. Jones confessed that initially she felt shame. Why proudly display a symbol of a country that didn't treat you as if you belonged? But her father, a military veteran, responded by telling his daughter that this nation belonged to him as much as to anyone else. He served this nation as a member of its armed services and would proudly display the flag of *his* country as he saw fit.

His response broadened Jones's perspective about the possibilities of Blackness and patriotism, and I think there's a lesson here for all of us, that we have to step away from the narrow constructs of national identity that were placed upon us by white supremacy. As I also asserted in my discussion of the Jezebel-Mammy paradigm, we must step away from constructs that suffocate us, that limit our expansiveness. I submit that Jones's experience can challenge us to think more deeply about our relationship with the flag as well as our broader connection to American symbols, songs, labels, and identity. It took me well into adulthood to realize that the choices being presented about Black national identity, about these codes of patriotism, were limited and destructive, that I could say "fuck that" and shape my national identity however I wanted. I could elevate Black life and consciousness and be a patriotic American.

Patriotic doublespeak is pervasive in our country. To speak of "American values," as so many right-wing pundits like to do, is to speak of a white America where racial and ethnic diversity can only be tolerated if these communities remain a numerical minority and adhere to traditional white, patriarchal standards of power, family, and identity. To make matters worse, white nationalist types have hijacked the American flag as the new Confederate flag, a universal symbol of white supremacy utilized to incite Black fear. And therefore the multitudes of Black people denying the Americanness that we feel in our bones plays right into white supremacist hands. For these people, an all-white nation, or at least a nation where Black people remain permanently subordinate, would be a dream.

BET ON BLACK

Rabble-rousing Black people pushing for equality and highlighting structural injustice are most certainly seen as an affront to so-called American values. The case of former NFL quarterback Colin Kaepernick is a prime example of this. In 2016, reporters started to notice that when the national anthem played, the 49ers player remained on the bench as a form of protest against police brutality and racial injustice. Kaepernick would eventually take the knee military-style during the anthem as a form of protest. And some white people immediately saw this act as a form of national disrespect, not considering that Kaepernick was exercising his constitutional right to make a statement in his land of birth, as President Barack Obama rightly pointed out. White folks were ready to throw the brother under the bus for taking their country to task without acknowledging that it was his country as well.

"The media painted this as I'm anti-American, anti-men and women of the military, and that's not the case at all," Kaepernick would say at a September 2016 news conference. I see his actions as embodying what James Baldwin said in his 1955 essay collection *Notes of a Native Son*: "I love America more than any other country in this world, and, exactly for this reason, I insist on the right to criticize her perpetually."

Kaepernick has it right, and Baldwin has it right: the right to protest, to demand that our nation be held accountable for the injustices it condones, can be a fundamental part of our national identity as Black people and thus pose no conflict with embracing our racial identity as well. To step back from our nationality would be a mistake, and so I encourage you to develop a mind-set that sees Americanness and devotion to country as a fundamental element of our Blackness.

Honestly, I didn't always feel this way. In fact, I was once a proponent of Black people having our own separate parcel of land in North America and couldn't have cared less whether we were viewed as being part of the United States. This hearkens back once again to my undergrad days at UNC when my Black studies classes were shaping my perspective in profound ways. Dr. Perry Hall, my professor who specialized in freewheeling advice, was also a serious scholar who spent much time imagining what Black liberation could look like in radical, nontraditional contexts. His thoughts were front and center in the Diaspora Studies course that he taught. Activist Marcus Garvey and his Universal Negro Improvement Association came up as part of our classroom focus, and the Pan-African leader's ideas around liberation intrigued me.

Activist Marcus Garvey believed that in a perfect world, the US government would have sent the formerly enslaved back to Africa because there was never a real plan for Black people to live in America as fully liberated first-class citizens, not even after Lincoln supposedly emancipated us.

Garvey essentially believed, since we weren't sent back, that we should marshal our economic resources collectively and go back to Africa under our own power. (From 1820 to 1864, anywhere from 11,000 to 16,000 freed Black Americans opted to move to the African nation of Liberia.) And if that wasn't a viable option, then America should just give Black people our own state with fifteen or twenty years of federal financing. Garvey's dreams would only come to fruition in a limited way, as he was convicted of fraud and deported to his home country of Jamaica. And no Black Americans ever traveled back to Africa under the auspices of Garvey's Universal Negro Improvement Association. But this idea of finding power in relocation and movement continues to capture the imagination of Black people everywhere in the diaspora.

During my undergrad days, I embraced this concept of Black people having our own state and had in fact identified Florida as the ideal place for our collective relocation. Florida has ports, resources, oranges, moderate weather, and continual sun, so I thought, *We could really, really rock some shit there. We could create a decent life and thrive economically.*

But over the years, through more reading, more education, and my lived experience, my positioning here has changed. I'm not willing to concede our place in our nation. The United States is as much Black folks' as it is white America's. And so I would position some of my ideas from my college days as the by-product of a passionate political consciousness mixed with youthful naivete.

(Interestingly, though my positioning back then seemed radical to most, some of my friends are now starting to get where I was coming from. An undergrad pal of mine from UNC, Lorenna, who's still my friend to this day, once said, "I thought you were so crazy and extreme back then when we were kids, but you know, Eboni, maybe you were on to something." She's given more credence to alternative options for our liberation; to her, mainstream integration increasingly seems like a fool's errand considering the continual bigotry Black people face generations after our so-called emancipation.)

Let's be clear: this notion of Black folks seeking refuge, opportunity, and a sense of peace via relocation—whether by going abroad or staying in America—is a fundamental part of our history and a very normal part of the Black experience. The Great Migration, where over the course of decades millions of Black citizens moved from the South to northern and western regions of America, was the largest mass movement of people in the United States in the twentieth century. As chronicled by Pulitzer Prize–winning journalist Isabel Wilkerson in her book *The Warmth of Other Suns*, this movement was spurred on by folks who weren't only looking for work opportunities but who were also refugees fleeing from a state-sanctioned system of deadly violence and oppression that included lynching, Jim Crow laws, and sharecropping.

Yet more recently there's been a shift after generations of movement to the North, which in fact had its own systems of discrimination and oppression, as many of y'all know. A reverse Great Migration has begun to occur. Finding themselves priced out of the real estate markets of expensive northern and western cities, Black folks are moving back down south, with 2020 census data showcasing that we're relocating to southern cities. For the first time in history, the greater Houston and Dallas–Fort Worth regions have more than one million Black residents. And according to a 2021 *Washington Post* report, most Black people are moving back to the South for economic reasons while also preferring to live among others who share the same racial identity as a safeguard against racism. In his *The Devil You Know: A Black Power Manifesto*, *New York Times* columnist Charles M. Blow asserts that Black people engaging in these migratory patterns have the right idea. He believes that members of our community who live in northern America should move to the South in order to form a massive political bloc that would allow us to call the shots as a cohesive, consolidated coalition.

But regardless of the racism we face, I believe it's important for Black people to honor just how much we've contributed to America's foundation and continual development.

The rejection of a Black-centered American patriotism has and continues to devastate our nation. White people might or might not be aware of this truth, but time's up on Black people being ostracized, excluded, and disinvited from American patriotism. And it's worthwhile to have conversations with our white peers about their place in redefining what it is to be American. If white Americans are serious about patriotism, they should be wholeheartedly antiracist in all of their daily practices. Why? Because it's in America's best interest to be "one nation," even when taking into account the level of diversity that the country has, even when considering how people of color have been routinely relegated to lower castes. A "one nation" America is a safer America, a more economically stable America, a more academically competent America, and a generally healthier America.

So to our fellow Americans who remain intent on denying Black people full access to our patriotism, to a first-class American experience, I believe we should say only one thing: it's too late. Time's up on denying us our national identity. We're no longer going to be manipulated into a posture of shame when it comes to claiming America. We should boldly claim this nation as our own, saying it loudly and proudly, while forthrightly critiquing all the shit here that doesn't work in the interest of a fully liberated Black economic, educational, and political existence. Because that's what's required for us to truly be one America.

BET ON BLACK

And one America means *all* Americans doing what's in the best interest of the entire nation. That means white people no longer get to monopolize who gets to identify as American. Black people have been American since there was the very first establishment of America. White people don't get the benefit of continuing to do fuck shit in their self-serving interest of pushing Black people out of our nation, whether rhetorically or literally. This is coming from a person who legitimately felt (and still feels) that Garvey was on to something. I still think the back to Africa movement has valid elements, but our approach to such a concept must holistically acknowledge who we are. Perhaps going to Africa means exploring our ancestral roots, coming to understand elements of culture that have shaped the Black American experience, and forging meaningful, nuanced connections across the diaspora. For those who are interested in permanently going back to the motherland, do you, boo, do you, but do so while being aware of the contemporary realities of the continent instead of looking for a mythical Shangri-La. And be mindful that your perspective on the world, how you move through spaces, has been shaped by your experiences as a Black American.

Let me also take a moment here to speak to more international communities, as I know there are plenty of Black people in America who migrated here from other lands. For that, I'm thankful. All of the ideas I've espoused about Black

168

patriotism apply to you as well, regardless of your legal status as a citizen or resident. If you're contributing economically to this country in some way, you have every right to have a say in its function and direction. At the same time, I ask that you don't do the work of white supremacy and further oppress Blackness by adopting language that positions Black Americans as being lazy and generally unsound compared to people from the Caribbean or Africa. This is a particularly egregious sentiment to hear, as any opportunities that Black immigrants to America might enjoy were created through the efforts of Black Americans over the centuries.

If you're an immigrant here, just do you and explore the possibilities of Blackness. You don't need to co-opt a Black American experience if you're not down for that, and you certainly don't need to support white supremacy with demeaning, ill-informed language about Black Americans. Just continue to operate at a fully liberated capacity as a Black person whether you're American or not. Just love being Black. Don't be bamboozled or hoodwinked into minimizing your Blackness in hopes that it'll get you anywhere in this nation, because I assure you, it will not.

Suffice it to say, many Black Americans are patriots, or at the very least are yearning to more avowedly declare our patriotism. We're as entitled to a strong and proud American identity as anyone else. And that proud claiming of America can also include searing critiques of our nation's flaws, especially when it's affected our well-being for generations. We can boldly critique all the shit that doesn't work in the interest of a fully liberated Black economic, educational, and political existence. That's what's required for us to truly be one nation, where white people no longer get to monopolize who identifies as real Americans. It is undisputed that unless and until Black people get good and goddamned ready to say otherwise, America is our country. And if white people are truly the patriots they claim to be, they'll move entirely according to the best interest of our country. There's only way to move forward in the national interest: a united America, an America that creates a patriotism speaking to the full, multifaceted possibilities of our country.

CHAPTER 6

LEVERAGE

"I believe that entrepreneurship is the ultimate smart money move and the surest path toward wealth for African Americans. Far fewer blacks than whites benefit from inherited wealth or assets. Entrepreneurship is the primary way to create the sort of wealth that can be passed on and built upon by succeeding generations."

—EARL G. GRAVES SR.

I T'S REALLY, *REALLY* HARD TO BE free when you don't own anything. I'll say it one more time, to let it sink in like it needs to. It's really hard to be free when you don't own anything. And yeah, I get it. Y'all might have been thinking that I've been talking in this book about our personal liberation and nuanced notions of patriotism in a more esoteric, abstract way, that I've been primarily focusing on individual and collective mind-sets as opposed to the material, nitty-gritty practical fundamentals of liberation. But don't get it twisted. I'm well aware that our freedom is deeply intertwined with our ability to own assets in America and share these resources with future generations of Black folks.

This notion of how important ownership is becomes easy to comprehend when you understand Black emancipation. We know for a fact that one of the ways in which Black people liberated themselves from slavery was by saving money that they earned, that is, if they were fortunate enough to find themselves in circumstances where they could work for actual wages as opposed to being forced to toil. This meant nonstop hustling, if you will, renting themselves out to do factory work or iron work or shoemaking or cabinetmaking or whatever skills that they may have obtained during the course of their life. If they were truly fortunate, they could save much of that money after paying their enslavers a monthly fee and literally buy their own freedom, potentially buying the freedom of their family members as well.

Let's be clear: these were woefully unjust circumstances and Black folks should *never* have had to pay for their legal emancipation at a time when white male property owners were given agency to do as they would throughout the land. Yet at the same time, as I continued to study the conditions of our ancestors, I began to understand the literal correlation between liberation, emancipation, and ownership in the United States. If you could earn enough old currency and build wealth to a certain extent, you could literally purchase your liberation, and this dynamic should illustrate to us how financial stability and security are essential to a first-class Black American experience.

It saddens me that I've had to gain lessons around money and resources from the time of slavery. My lessons in understanding the importance of wealth have involved a long, winding path, even though I had early examples in my family of entrepreneurship, particularly when it came to having multiple streams of income. Growing up, my mother, Gloria, would often tell me stories about my grandpa Cary Williams Sr. He bagged feed for horses, cows, and other animals in southeast Louisiana as his primary paycheck job while cutting hair on the side from his porch. And then on the side-side he sold booze. So he was basically running a bar, running a barbershop, and handling feed for livestock. Oh, and I should also mention he trimmed lawns for cemeteries on the weekends.

My mother duplicated the example her father set for generating multiple revenue streams. So when she was in beauty school, attending classes with the goal of opening her own salon, she drove a Charlotte-Mecklenburg school bus at five o'clock in the morning. She worked for UPS in the evenings, and then on the weekends she would drive an airport shuttle that took fliers from short-term or long-term parking to their terminal. After opening her salon, my mom went on to open a chain of day care facilities and also operated, of all things, a tractor-trailer business. She was the first Black woman that I knew of in the South who owned and operated her own tractor-trailer company, eventually having a fleet of three trucks. My mother has always been strategic about these things. She thought, if a recession hits, people may not be able to afford the luxury of getting their hair done every week for twenty bucks. And so opening a day care facility made sense because no matter what happens to the economy, most folks will still need to have someone watch their kids. No matter what happens to the economy, goods are going to have to get from point A to point B.

Like a lot of folks, most people in my family worked hard. We knew how to make money and hustle hard, but what my family had never learned how to do was to create and build wealth. Earning money is quite different from wealth building. I don't want to shame my family here, but I do want to tell the truth. After all the hard work my grandfather did, and after all the tremendous work my mother has done, the amount of intergenerational assets we have access to as a family doesn't reflect their toil. Earning money is all about making enough to make ends meet (hopefully) and enjoy the elements of life, while wealth building is all about owning financial assets that you can rely on until you die, eventually passing said assets on to forthcoming generations.

Post-slavery, the United States has done its best to economically disenfranchise Black communities. This has created a wealth gap that has remained in place for decades, with Black families on average having far less wealth than our white counterparts. According to the nonpartisan policy institute the Center for American Progress, in 2019 the average Black household had $142,330 in wealth as compared to $980,549 for the average white household. In other words, Black households had merely 14.5 percent on average of the wealth of white households. The reasons for this are multifold. Black people were denied access to the same homeownership opportunities that our white counterparts had, due to everything from legal redlining practices, where we were forced to live in less desirable areas throughout the country, to predatory lending schemes that we faced throughout the twentieth century. This crippled our opportunity to build wealth in our communities, as homeownership has long been seen as the primary way of building wealth in America. We've also faced work discrimination, which affects our economic outlook, and have been offered lower wages for the same work done by white people. The obstacles to financial equity and wealth building are real, and they must be stated here as we continue to grapple with their pervasive legacy. But we can't wait for white people to miraculously come to their senses and do the right thing. We must create our own opportunities for wealth building with the resources that are afforded to us and that we have on our own.

Even without having access to any real wealth as a kid, I was taken care of in some ways. Because of my academic accomplishments in high school, I had people and organizations that invested in my education. Thus I was blessed to graduate from the University of North Carolina at Chapel Hill on a full merit scholarship without undergraduate debt, later taking on law school debt that I'm still paying back.

BET ON BLACK MOVE

VIEW YOUR EDUCATION AS AN INVESTMENT

It may go without saying that investing in a college or university education is a generally solid path to improving one's job prospects and obtaining a quality of life in which wealth building becomes easier. But don't get it twisted: you still need to be mindful of how much you're spending on your education and what your prospects will be based on the degree you attain. Before you go into major debt for the sake of an undergraduate degree or pursue an advanced degree, for that matter, ask yourself: What will be my earning potential upon graduation? Is the degree I'm going for worth all that I'm going to pay in terms of recouping my investment? Is there a cheaper way to cultivate a particular skill set? Do I really need to go to the super expensive school to be competitive in the job market? And what scholarships or fellowships can I apply for?

I know lots of people still say that a liberal arts education is all about exploring your passions, making connections, and feeling free to connect with one's heart's desire and all that lah-di-dah bullshit. And yes, that ideally should be part of the experience of Blackness, where college course-work is fueled primarily by one's passions and interests. I'll admit, I focused on Black studies in college because it was my heart's desire to do so, but I still had a plan, receiving academic scholarships with my sight set on law school from an early age. All that to say, I'm cognizant of the reality of our situation, that so many of us are coming from more humble circumstances where money is limited. We often need to think strategically about how much we're going to invest in college so that we're relatively unencumbered when it comes to creating future wealth for ourselves and our communities.

I've subsequently had all sorts of ups and downs with my salary, starting with a six-figure corporate law firm job before I took a major pay cut to be a public defender. I eventually moved away from law altogether, relocating to LA to build a media career while working dead-end jobs. Fast-forward to 2014 when I began to work for CBS News, and I can honestly say from that point on I've had legitimately high earnings every year. And yet it wasn't until 2022, at the age of thirty-eight, that I would purchase my first tangible asset, a home in Harlem.

I've developed a somewhat recent obsession with the Black wealth gap in this nation and understanding its causes and what we can do about it. I used to be really lackadaisical around the reparations conversation, saying things like, "Of course they owe us money and opportunity. Of course it would be nice to receive, but realistically speaking, it's not gonna happen, so let's just move on." But more recently I've been like, "Bitch, just what are you talking about? Like no, they need to give us our dough, like yesterday." It's time to explore what the reparations package needs to look like. I maintain that real estate and education are two of the most appreciable assets in modern America that Black people could use as a bedrock for closing wealth gaps and ensuring our perennial liberation as Black people in America.

I'm not trying to give y'all a lecture, but my spiel about owning assets and wealth building is more of a cautionary tale, with yours truly as the misguided protagonist of the story. I really didn't focus on wealth with everything I had at the beginning of my career, and I was most certainly on the path of becoming yet another high-earning, overeducated, financially struggling individual, a plight that's all too common in our culture. There were times in my life when I'd literally made over $300,000 or $400,000 a year and I didn't own shit other than the clothes on my back. That type of mind-set was and is completely unacceptable for a fully liberated Black existence. I don't want you to be another person working their fingers to the bone night and day, proudly displaying a certain type of work ethic and mode of Black excellence and ultimately having nothing to show for it by way of actual tangible wealth.

And to be clear, the point of having wealth and assets isn't to just be another rich bitch for the sake of flashing fly shit for the world to see. Might feel good, but it's not really where you want to go. That fly shit mentality in fact often gets in the way of us building wealth. We've got to do away with this continual push to have a luxury lifestyle when we could be saving money to invest in the stock market or property or our own business enterprise. No, the point of the wealth is to have the access and the opportunity to buy our own liberation, to buy freedom in a world that for better or for worse operates under a capitalistic system. When you have access to assets, it allows you to make decisions about your life direction and general well-being that you wouldn't otherwise be able to make.

And that is the quest I want you to be on, to center ownership as much as you can in everything that you do. Ownership of my media endeavors has been a cornerstone of me being able to build wealth in a way that speaks both to my professional passions and sociopolitical sensibilities. Let's look at my podcast *Holding Court*, which debuted in 2020. The show marked the first time that I really took ownership of something as part of my career. One reason I entered into a deal with Black Effect, Charlamagne, and the iHeart team for the podcast is that the terms were amenable to my own financial interests and, most important, because I would retain ownership rights. Other media companies were most certainly interested in the podcast, but I wouldn't enter into a deal with these clients because they required full ownership of an intellectual property that *I* had created and would host. And that just wasn't going to work for me. If I hadn't learned anything else in the past few years, I knew that I couldn't give away my ownership rights like that, not considering all that those who'd come before had survived. When it comes to business deals, always be real fucking curious when people don't want you to have something.

Ownership might mean getting less money up front for a deal where you retain at least partial ownership as compared to what you might get if you sold away your rights to a show. But on the real, have faith that you'll make it up in the long run, that the passion that you'll put into running your own business will yield future financial rewards.

The concept of ownership has to be paramount for us Black folks. There's a paradigm shift going on culturally that says we're centering ownership. So that's why I'm challenging you to routinely exercise discipline. It takes discipline to center ownership, which is one of the reasons that it took so long for *Holding Court* to come back for a second season. We had a very successful first season but ended up being off the air for almost a year. As a content creator, it was fuckin' terrible to wait that long to get my ass back on the air and offer legal analysis to my audience. I missed my own show, and I certainly heard from listeners who were like, "Where are you?" I could have easily just done another deal, but I had to exercise discipline and engage in negotiations that would elevate my stakes and ownership of the show. It was essential, and it was the only way I could proceed with this work in good conscience.

And let's be real, y'all, Auntie E loves her some money on the table. You better believe it from my reaction to the people who were running over to negotiate long-term contracts with *Holding Court* and offering a lot of money. But these same entities wanted to fully own my intellectual property, and I simply couldn't allow that. So I had to use discipline and forego instant gratification for the sake of making a clearheaded, principled ownership-centered decision.

I know some of y'all might be reading this and saying to yourself, "Well, that's good for you, Eboni, but I'm not in a position to negotiate with 'moneyed companies' to start a business." Or you're like, "I don't have capital of my own to invest in a business." And I say in response, "It's all good. These same principles of discipline and centeredness can work for you regardless of your work status." Earl G. Graves Sr., who passed in 2020, was the esteemed founder of the magazine *Black Enterprise*, among other endeavors, and published the 1997 book *How to Succeed in Business without Being White: Straight Talk on Making It in America.* The man was brilliant at what he did, maintaining a conscience while facing the reality of Black circumstances in America and speaking to workers at all levels. "To have a successful career, you have to approach it as an entrepreneur, even if you are working for someone else," Graves once said. "Your career is your own private business. You have to market yourself and your abilities and knowledge just as you would a product or service."

In other words, to have a successful career, you have to approach it as a disciplined entrepreneur, even if you're working for someone else, even if your career is in fact more of a job. Your career is your own private business, and so you can thoughtfully position and highlight your abilities and knowledge, just as you might a product or service, in a way that can more likely lead to career advancement or at the very least cultivate the type of work life you want to have. I would offer that holding this type of attitude about your work is key to developing entrepreneurial opportunities as you see fit, and it's certainly conducive to having a more satisfactory professional life. Just please say no to coming to your job with any sort of attitude or projecting all of your emotional life stuff into business or your place of work. As a Black person, let your vision, your needs, and your desire to achieve inform how you show up for work and what your expectations for yourself will be.

Let's say you're going into an office every day, working 9 to 5. What are the choices you're making with the income you're receiving? Are you able to put aside money to build assets simultaneously so that ownership can absolutely still take place in some way, whether it's saving for a down payment on a home or cultivating an investment portfolio in the stock market? Let's think of the ways in which choice was ruthlessly stripped from our ancestors, and let that inform our path. You should constantly be centering ownership in your path, in your process, in your approach to the money you earn and the way you show up in spaces. Doing so is an integral component of Blackness.

When it comes to ownership, creativity and flexibility are supreme, which we as Black people have specialized in in order to survive the Western world. When you think about what asset building looks like, for instance, a lot of us live in cities and metropolises that make homeownership feel out of reach. And this is where creativity and flexibility come in. As of this writing, the average house in New York City is essentially a million dollars, and the average first-time home buyer in New York still has to put down 20 percent on said property. The realities of this type of market are cost prohibitive for tons of people. It was almost cost prohibitive to me when it came to purchasing my house, even with my salary, and I don't mind saying that out loud.

When I say that we need to get creative, I mean exploring ideas like checking out the co-op and condo markets if a smaller space could work for you or thinking about the notion of some kind of collaborative buy. If you're clear that your earnings and the amount of cash you have on hand won't be sufficient for a home down payment and a hefty mortgage, see if there's someone in your life with whom you could purchase the property together. Is the home large enough so that you could essentially have separate living spaces if you want to maintain a certain level of privacy and autonomy? Or would it be fine to share a living room, kitchen, and bathroom in a standard two-bedroom unit? There would, of course, be lots of things you'd need to discuss legally before going into such a venture with someone, and there'd most certainly be tons of red tape, but exploring these types of options is better than the latter. And on top of this, you'd be working together, combining your resources so that you can both work toward generating wealth for yourselves and the Black community.

Another thing to keep in mind is that you don't necessarily have to live in the place you own. You can buy a whole house in Mississippi, Alabama, or Louisiana at much more affordable prices than you would find in more dense urban markets in the North and West. My father did this, purchasing a whole fucking house for $70,000 cash in Montgomery, Alabama. So that's another option that I think we need to be thinking about as Black people. If we can't buy in Atlanta, Chicago, Washington, DC, or New York, can we buy in Texas? Can we buy in South Carolina and have a potentially profitable rental property?

My point here is that it's imperative for us to play with this concept of ownership, to allow the versatility, craftiness, and ingenuity that allowed us to survive under adverse circumstances to dictate our financial growth. Be flexible and open, but by all means, invest in your own beautiful, bountiful future.

CHAPTER 7
PROCESS

"Without commitment, you'll never start, but more importantly, without commitment, you'll never finish... Keep working, keep striving, never give up, fall down seven times, get up eight... Ease is a greater threat to progress than hardship, so keep moving, keep growing, keep learning. See you at work."

—DENZEL WASHINGTON

W E'VE ALMOST REACHED THE END of our foray into Blackness…for now. I certainly hope it's been as rewarding for you to read as it's been for me to share my thoughts. But I couldn't end this narrative without going fully into an idea that's near and dear to my heart, that I believe is essential for Black folks to adopt when it comes to setting ourselves up for success: namely, fully honoring the process involved in getting from point A to B and then C, the process that will ideally lead you to a place of success, grace, and power.

When I've appeared on *The View* or my podcast *Holding Court*, people often remark how comfortable I am on-air or sitting at the table with a group of other women, leaning into cultural gab or political topics while centering my Blackness. My first stint as guest host on *The View* began in October of 2021, and the general consensus, even from the critics, was that Eboni crushed it, she killed it. She looked like she was always there, like she'd been at that table for years. Having appeared a couple more times on the show since then, the feedback I hear is that I'm a natural, that I innately possess the qualities necessary to be a competent, poised host.

Ha, ha. Bitch, *please*. If they only knew the truth about the toil, sweat, tears, and insecurity I've experienced before getting to that table. The fact of the matter is that I've put in years of work and training to exude a certain level of confidence and professionalism, that it didn't come naturally or without effort. Rather, it took much time, and the poise that people are responding to is a direct result of the long, extended process of doing what I needed to do in a variety of professional arenas. I'd in fact long campaigned to appear on *The View* to no avail, and it wasn't until I'd become a Real Housewife that I got a call out of the blue to appear as a guest host on the show.

Different people will have different forms of process depending on who they are and the goals they've set for themselves, but honoring process is key to sustaining a sense of excellence, to achieving one's goals, to moving forward in life as you unapologetically center your Blackness. Process is about doing the work, consistently, sustainably, long term, no bullshit, no complaints.

When it comes to my law career, which continues to inform my work as a podcaster and journalist, we're talking about a fifteen-year professional process between my practicing law from a base preliminary level to an elite level. There's been a similar process with my media career, going from, you know, greener than a green bean to what I think most of my colleagues would consider being an elite broadcaster.

And even at this stage of the game, I'm still not above the process. Nobody is above the process. This is why at the beginning of this chapter I called out that famous quote from actor Denzel Washington's NAACP Image Award acceptance speech for *Fences* in 2017. His words are all about keeping things moving no matter what you've achieved or how stellar your peers think you are. Keep improving, even upon excellence, and stay in the process.

In addition to Denzel, another popular performer greatly affected my understanding of the value of process, a performer I believe didn't get his flowers as quickly as others because of his sexuality. And it's Billy Porter. The oh-so-divine Porter is indisputably one of the most skilled and talented artists of our time, having won a Tony, a Grammy, and an Emmy (he just needs that Oscar) for work ranging from the Broadway musical *Kinky Boots* to the TV show *Pose*. The Carnegie Mellon graduate became the first openly queer man to win a prime-time Emmy before going on to publish his memoir and directing a rom-com starring a trans actress. He's an unadulterated, A-list superstar, and has the hardware to prove it.

I saw Billy Porter and *Pose* producer/showrunner Ryan Murphy at a talk at the 92nd Street Y circa 2018. I was at a critical crossroads at the time, because I was in the process of leaving Fox and I didn't know what was next. I was very frustrated because I felt like things were supposed to go great with my career, that I should've been setting myself up to be the best in the business. But it wasn't happening. I'd even had the chance to host a prime-time news show, but it didn't work out. I didn't feel like I was where I deserved to be after all of my toil and sacrifice.

But as I sat in this theater on the Upper East Side of New York, my expectations were checked. Billy went on to explain that he was a big, grown fifty-plus-year-old man who'd been working effectively in the business for over thirty years, doing Broadway, off Broadway, local theater, ba-ba-ba-ba... and then, and then finally, finally, with *Pose*, he's achieved success? Even with all his accolades in the theatrical world, Porter regularly dealt with all aspects of the industry saying things like, "You're too gay. You're halfway, not gay enough. You're certainly too Black. You're too churchy. You're too gospel . . ." Even after he won the Tony for *Kinky Boots* and blew up the Broadway industry, Porter couldn't get a role. It was like all of that drama and fire and applause, the assumption he held that he'd made it, and then radio silence. Crickets. And then several fucking years pass before he lands *Pose*, and people are like, "Oh, my God! Billy Porter, you know, he's such a wonder. And he just came out of nowhere!" Ignorant.

But the reality is this: Porter had been doing the work at an elite, exceptional level for decades before really getting his due, and as he told his story, I realized I needed to check myself. Eboni K. Williams, for all the legitimacy of your argument about wanting to make it within a certain time frame, who the fuck are you? If *Billy fucking Porter* of all people had to wait thirty years for his moment, for his big break with *Pose*, I needed to sit my ass down, put my head down, and get back to work.

So I gradually made peace with where I was with my career and continued to move forward, learning lessons from past experiences. And when I eventually got to that *View* chair, I was far wiser and more aware than when I was more of a fledgling broadcaster, when I simply wouldn't have been ready.

And if I'm honest with myself, if I'd had more insight and foresight when I was going through what I was going through with my career, I would've realized that I've always taken the more circuitous route when it comes to my career. Let me take y'all back a bit, and give ya'll more insight into the early media career of Auntie E, which in many ways epitomizes this concept of process. While still in my twenties, I left a corporate law firm in Raleigh-Durham, North Carolina, to move to California in the hope of making it in the media business. Unable to practice law in any other way besides handling doc reviews, with some modeling and print work insufficient to pay the bills on their own, I also ended up having to do a lot of odd jobs. Believe it or not I was a bottle service girl at times. In other words, I was the young woman who reaches out to you at the door at the nightclub and says, "Do you want Grey Goose or Johnnie Walker?"

Up until this time, I hadn't realized how much being a lawyer had been a part of my identity. There was a potential paradox here: even though I had been very intentional with my decision to go to law school, wanting the credentials for almost as long as I could remember, I had also never thought of myself as one of those lawyers who needed to throw what I did for a living and what I had accomplished in people's faces. That just felt way too obnoxious and pretentious to me, and I still wore my Ponderosa roots on my sleeve. So before moving to LA, when asked about my job, I would simply respond, "I work at the courthouse" or "I'm an advocate." But when I couldn't practice law to support myself in a new city, I was humbled, and it made me realize how much my professional achievements meant to me.

But I eventually got my big break by entering talk radio through a mutual connection and ended up working at KFI

AM 640, which was the largest conservative radio station in Southern California. Their sister station used to be the home base for Rush Limbaugh and Sean Hannity. KFI was also home for entertainment industry pro, media commentator, and writer Mo'Kelly, the only Black man with a show at the station who was also kind of independent in his political thinking. Mo needed somebody to come on and do legal analysis for the case of Jodi Arias, a woman who was ultimately convicted in 2013 of murdering her ex-boyfriend, Travis Alexander, in a particularly grisly way. I'd never done radio before and had never thought of radio as an entryway into the media world, being more geared toward television opportunities. And I wasn't so thrilled about KFI's conservative orientation. But something in my spirit told me not to turn down this opportunity, that there was something there.

I soon started going on Mo's show regularly as a legal analyst. It was actually quite rewarding to bypass the glitz and glam that I had so long seen as by-products of the media world. With radio, you had to rely primarily on your preparation for a story. You had to rely on making legal vernacular clear to a wide audience. You had to rely on your words and your ability to tell a story and convey nuanced analysis with only your words. All that I've just described here added up to one thing: process. I was developing the skill sets that would be invaluable for my future career.

I was eventually able to negotiate having my own segment on his show, which would be called "Celebrity Justice with Eboni K. Williams," and it would air every Friday. My fledgling radio career became the beginning of me, or rather the me that would eventually become known to audiences nationwide. It was an ironic setup. I was a conscious, educated, intellectually leaning Black woman entering a professional space that wasn't designed for me, and so I had to figure out how to make this opportunity work while honoring who I knew myself to be.

I look back at my entry into KFI as a really bold move, especially as I wasn't planning to go to California to break into conservative talk radio. It all appeared to be quite happenstance, but this is where, for me, I refer to my belief in the invisible hand of God. I believe in divine order, in the divine ordering of steps. This was, in retrospect, God orchestrating the training ground for my future work. Talk radio was how I first learned to position myself properly in front of a microphone. It's how I first learned to craft legal, political, and economic arguments that could pierce through a lot of ideological partisan bullshit conversation and that could help make a difference in the lives of others, skills that would serve me well later in my broadcast career. After time spent in Los Angeles limbo, I was relieved to once again be a full-fledged legal advocate, and I used a practical approach in delivering my legal analysis for the sake of strategically cutting through the partisan noise. I was also gaining first-hand understanding of the power of radio, learning how sociopolitical movements could be consolidated to create an airwave behemoth, something that I dearly wish more liberal channels could understand.

By the time I was offered guest hosting opportunities by the station, I felt relatively confident in the advice I was offering to listeners even if my long-term road map for a broadcasting career felt less clear. I ended up taking on guest hosting duties multiple times a week, which was how I was starting to get a bit of a reputation as a bright on-air personality and getting media hits.

I was still with Mo's show as well, two years having passed.

As it so happened, while I was building up my profile on KFI, I'd also started moonlighting with the NFL. I've never been one to put all my eggs in one basket, even when things are going well. So while doing the radio thing I continued to network. I eventually reconnected with Mark Watts, a onetime mentor of mine who had reached out to my mother to get an update on my whereabouts. Once she put us in touch, I learned he was working as head of talent at the NFL Network.

When I first met with Mark, relaying to him my original idea to be an on-screen personality, he was blunt with his assessment. He knew I wasn't ready for TV, but he was patient, taking time out to show me the ropes and helping me to transition my radio skills to television skills. Mark was such a pro, and his gift to me was that he showed me how to become what he called a total broadcaster, or someone whose messaging, effectiveness, and communication are consistent across all platforms. So whether you're a guest on the radio or anchoring the local news on TV or hosting a national talk show, or you're writing a newspaper op-ed or crafting a long-form online article or authoring a memoir, your identity must be consistently maintained throughout all endeavors. So whoever Eboni K. Williams is on KFI is whoever Eboni K. Williams is on *The Breakfast Club* is whoever Eboni K. Williams is on *The View* is whoever Eboni K. Williams is on *Medium*. And if any of that is out of sync, you're not a total broadcaster and you have work to do. Pre-TV, that became one of my preliminary benchmarks of success, to be a total broadcaster all the time, to maintain the discipline that doing so would entail.

And soon I was ready, though I wasn't remotely expecting to cover the case that would produce my first television opportunity. One night I got a call around ten thirty from Mark saying that the NFL Network needed an analyst to cover the Aaron Hernandez trial. As many of you already know, Hernandez was a player for the New England Patriots who'd been indicted for murder, and the station needed a lawyer to come in and explain the case to their audience. You have to remember, this is the NFL Network, which is owned by the league itself. So the powers that be were extremely nervous to even have a discussion about Hernandez on their network, but they knew they had to do it, considering that one of their players was going to face an unprecedented amount of public scrutiny. That was quite a bit of pressure to suddenly bear as a rookie legal analyst for TV. But though I was nervous, I knew I had to seize the opportunity. Since I'd gotten the call at ten thirty, this meant I needed to be at the studio and camera ready by three o'clock that morning. This was because the show was taped on the West Coast but aired at six o'clock in the morning on the East Coast. So, in 2012, I made my first national TV appearance.

My coverage of the case went well, and I soon started to receive follow-up calls from producers asking for my analysis on what was happening, for instance, with Colin Kaepernick and his protests or some other controversy that could blow up in the league's face. It stayed this way for around eight months, where I would be getting ready for dinner or be out with my sorority sisters or, heaven forbid, on a date, and then the call would come at like nine thirty or ten o'clock. So then I'd have to apologize to whomever I was hanging with, go take a nap, pop back up at midnight, do my own hair and makeup, and get to the studio in Culver City to create live content.

And there were no shortcuts to making this happen. One thing you cannot bypass on a pathway to true excellence is the process. There're so many people who want the glory, who want the blue checkmark on their Instagram profile, who deeply crave the attention and celebrity and the related rewards. But are you taking time to quietly develop your skill sets with mentors for the opportunities that will inevitably come? Are you taking the ten o'clock phone calls at night to be live in the studio several hours later in the early morning and then getting yourself together? Are you observing, learning, asking questions, making mistakes, and then correcting those mistakes? That was the process. And I tell young people that I don't really want to hear the bullshit and the whining until you've proven you're committed to the process of achieving whatever it is you know in your bones you're meant to achieve. If you're expecting something from an experience and you're not adequately pouring yourself—your energy, your enthusiasm, your thoughtfulness, your time—into the experience, you deserve nothing from it. This is how I was raised and how I continue to operate.

Nobody is above the process. When faced with challenges, get back to work, keep improving, even upon excellence, and stay in the process. And yes, I know some would argue that it's unfair that many Black folks presumably have a longer process when it comes to achieving greatness due to structural racism and the anti-Black biases of our systems. These are valid arguments and I applaud those who are directly doing the work of trying to change these structures. But I was raised to never get caught up with notions of fairness or deservedness. In general, I think notions of fairness are distracting and serve as red herrings when it comes to doing what we need to do as Black folks. Understand the situation, get mad, get fuckin' *pissed* if you need to, grieve over what you've lost because of structural biases, and then keep it moving, doing what you need to do for yourself and the community.

And please, as I mentioned in discussing my own efforts to be on *The View* and in reflecting on Billy Porter's career, don't sweat it when it comes to being rejected. Rejection will happen to you inevitably, and it will probably happen to you often in some shape or fashion, and we don't talk enough about that in our society. In our 24/7 social media era, people really like to amplify and share affirmations, successes, and wins. Look at me, I got this limited-edition Gucci bag. Look at me, I got this new bikini and I look hot wearing it. Look at me, I closed the deal on this badass movie campaign. Look at me, I got this new role, this new position, this new love…God knows, all of that's great. But you better believe that for anyone who's had any kind of success, underneath that success there's been far more rejection, a discomfiting part of the process that rarely gets shared on our shiny apps.

For instance, in 2022, I was fired not once, but twice. I want to be very transparent. *REVOLT Black News* technically fired me. The execs were grateful for my work on the platform as a host but had decided they were going to move in a different direction, placing their focus on the Atlanta market and skewing to a younger demo by hiring a younger host who they could also pay less. Blah, blah, blah…And you know, it was a bit uncomfortable, which is to be expected with any sort of letting-go procedure, but it was really okay. I wasn't fired because I wasn't excellent in my job. I was fired because the company needed to make a business decision that lowered their budget and spoke to a particular audience. And *RHONY* had also decided to go in a different direction with how they assembled their cast for their latest season, no doubt because I wasn't giving them standard Housewives hijinks. I didn't like it, but I got it, and it wasn't like losing these gigs meant that I wasn't going to keep on keeping on, doing what I needed to do for my career and for my spirit, and honoring my process. In fact, on the same night that I was told that I wouldn't be brought back for *RHONY*, I started working on a preproduction pitch sheet for my own reality show, *Harlem USA*, an enterprise where I knew I'd be able to center Blackness in myriad ways with no goddamned backchat.

BET ON BLACK MOVE

DON'T GIVE IN TO DESPERATION

I want to also touch on the topic of one's emotional state when it comes to dealing with work and life challenges, especially if you've been let go or haven't landed an opportunity and you're unsure about next steps. If there's a feeling of desperation around trying to hold on to or have access to something that you craved, that you thought for sure would be your thing, then maybe it's not for you. To be sure, those feelings of desperation, or what I call frantic energy, are difficult to cope with. This is that fast-beating heart, that obsessive line of thought that says, "If I can somehow get that position, get *anything*, I'll feel better." This is when you can't think of anything else. When you wake up in the morning and you go to sleep at night, and your psyche's occupied with, *Oh, I hope I get the call for that second interview round for that thing I applied to last week.* Or: *Oh, God, you know, I really, really hope I landed the audition and made the show.*

A lot of this has to do with tempo and energy. If you find yourself acting impulsively, constantly pacing, wholly unable to be still as you think about a potential opportunity, as if persistent magical thinking will somehow get you the job, those are signs of desperation. This is a sign that you're caught up in the false notion that this one job or this one role is the be-all and end-all of your existence. It's really just a sign of something not being in alignment, because again, for me, going to faith, I don't believe God wants you in a posture of desperation. I don't believe that God calls you to be in a state of frantic energy. I think God wants you to be operating from a place of peace and insight and abundance.

The moment you find yourself operating from a belief system that's rooted in scarcity—I don't care if we're talking about professional opportunities, romantic love, familial relationships, money, and so on—you are on the wrong path. It's very normal for anxiety to come up when you really want a position and need to feel stable. We're human. But it's not a good idea to make decisions based on anxiety. Trust the process and take a moment to let the anxiety pass, fully understanding the array of options that you actually have.

To be honest, 90 percent of my career has consisted of me hearing *no*. That fuckin', aggravating *no*. Yes, just like everyone else I'd like to kick it to the curb sometimes, but alas, it's a normal part of the process. If you get stuck in the *no*, and if you allow the *no* to dictate your self-perception, your qualifications, your worthiness, or even your skill set, you will put yourself in peril. You'll be allowing rejection to get in your head, potentially undermining your confidence, and causing a type of existential paralysis where you're not moving at all. Now, I'm not talking about having a lack of awareness about what elements of your skill set you might need to work on to improve your chances of getting work, and I think it's good to take an inventory. It's fine to self-assess and ask yourself, "Why is this opportunity getting away from me?" Sometimes a missed opportunity is indeed connected to performance or lack of professional experience. Maybe you didn't get chosen for that role as a manager at the café because your skill sets aren't quite right, and don't quite match the job. If that's the case, don't sweat it, and move on to the next venue. But oftentimes, it's not you as much as the circumstances of a particular organization or someone's subjective experience.

I'm putting this all out there because these are ideas I'd like for us all to grapple with, because doing so will give us the space to have a nuanced understanding of what it takes to make it. Others can offer "You can do it!" slogans, and sometimes we need to hear that, sure. But I want to make sure that my people are approaching our careers with depth and foresight. That's what I want for our expressions of Blackness, an approach to success that's informed by thoughtfulness and a holistic awareness that will cultivate our freedom.

CHAPTER 8

EVERYTHING

"You were born where you were born and faced the future that you faced because you were Black and for no other reason. The limits of your ambition were, thus, expected to be set forever. You were born into a society which spelled out with brutal clarity, and in as many ways as possible, that you were a worthless human being. You were not expected to aspire to excellence: you were expected to make peace with mediocrity."

—JAMES BALDWIN

YOU ARE QUALIFIED.

It's one of my favorite things to tell young people that I have the honor of mentoring, whether newly minted graduates from an HBCU or traveling abroad to Rwanda doing advocacy work, where I was honored to sit with a group of schoolgirls coming into their own and figuring out their individual voices. You are qualified. It's my mantra, my way of dispelling the messages we've received over the course of our lives that we're inferior, deserving of subordination, of being sidelined, of being cast away if we're not deemed useful to the dominant, white power structure. Such trash, such awful ideas. And so I am relentless when it comes to telling folks, *You are qualified...*

to do whatever it's in your heart and mind to do, to occupy space in whatever way you want to.

And yeah, I get it, even though I'm using this statement in the broadest sense possible, this idea of qualification most directly speaks to making one's way in the workplace. We think of ourselves as being qualified for a job based on our education, training, and previous professional experiences. And we share our qualifications by presenting our credentials to an employer to see if we're an ideal match for the job opportunity they're offering. Sounds straightforward enough, but this can actually be a fraught experience for Black folks, especially considering how often we're called upon to prove ourselves professionally in a way our white (and male) counterparts aren't. The immediate assumption is that what we'll bring to the table in terms of our skill set, knowledge base, and competency will be subpar.

But let's face it: any Black person who's made it to a particular position of power when it comes to their work is most likely overqualified in some way for that position. We've historically not benefited from belonging to networks of access that would allow us to get jobs based on others' perceived notions about our inability to fit into certain work cultures. We often don't get jobs based on who we know in the way that white people have been able to do for so long, regardless of how subpar their performance at school and previous jobs might have been. And please, don't just take your Auntie E's word on this. There are ample studies out there showcasing how Black folks are still discriminated against in the job market, including a 2021 study by economists from the University of California, Berkeley, and the University of Chicago that showed how résumés submitted with traditionally Black names got fewer callbacks from more than a hundred companies than job seekers with more white names.

Not only do Black people face hurdles when it comes to being hired, but we're held up to more rigid measures of performance than our white counterparts. According to Gillian B. White, a reporter for the *Atlantic*, a 2015 study found that Black workers are routinely overqualified for the positions we hold, and in fact this overqualification is what ensures that we get to keep the damn job in the first place. White notes, "In order to keep a job, black workers also must meet a higher bar. Only in instances where black workers are monitored and displayed a significantly higher skill level than their white counterparts would they stand a significant chance of keeping their jobs for a while...But even in instances where the productivity of black workers far exceeded their white counterparts, there was still evidence that discrimination persisted, which could lead to lower wages or slower promotions."

This is a bitter pill to swallow for sure, but it's also potentially empowering and part of the good news. We know the truth, that job structures in America have historically been racist. And thus affirmative action and diversity hire initiatives were put in place at the collective behest of our ancestors and elders to help correct this pattern of oppression. We can and should embrace the opportunities that these programs provide. Now some of y'all might be concerned about the expectation floating around among white colleagues that your skill set will be inferior because you were partially hired because you're a person of color. It's like being hired for your Blackness somehow eradicates all the years of hard work you've put in.

Well, I'm here to tell you just the opposite, that diversity hire and affirmative action programs are in fact a welcome tool when it comes to your pathway to greatness. I've understood for quite some time that this notion of being an inferior affirmative action or diversity hire candidate all comes from a lie created by white power structures. It comes from a willful misrepresentation of policies in order to maintain the status quo.

In this life, you will likely encounter jobs, people, peers, supervisors, and entire spaces that will work overtime to tell you in big ways and microscopic ways that you are *not* qualified. They will attempt to indict your credibility. They will attempt to bring down your confidence. They will poke and prod with interrogations about your major, your background, your school, your grade point average, and a number of other so-called indicators of success. And sadly, sometimes these instigators of disqualification look just like you and me.

They will do this in an attempt to make you question yourself. An attempt to make you doubt yourself. An attempt to make you shrink. And, ultimately, they do this in an effort to make you disqualify yourself.

They do this to take you out of the game before it even starts so that they can eliminate you as competition and essentially slip into their own mediocrity.

Whether you got the job because you met the qualifications (I repeat, you likely exceed them!) or via affirmative action or diversity protocols, who gives a damn?! The good news of today is that we know the only real antidote to this level of persistent prejudice in the workplace and within enterprise is to intentionally curate space for Black people. Companies know that such forms of oppression, racial biases, and innate anti-Blackness exist. That's what it's all about when they proclaim "diversity." It's a self-accountability model where those who control white spaces—and, to be clear, white spaces aren't exclusively policed by white people—can self-assess and say, "We see how anti-Blackness is showing up here and preventing qualified Black people from occupying this space. And as an organization or company or media enterprise, we're actually going to do something about it.

And what we're going to do is insist upon the occupancy of Blackness in this anti-Black space. We're going to intentionally insist upon the occupancy of qualified, capable Blackness." They know this shit is fucked up. And we can't let them forget it. We're going to get these jobs, slay opportunity, and proceed with power.

Dehumanizing Blackness is detrimental not only to Black people but to people in general. Even with the assumptions that have been made about my being a diversity hire, my work isn't about shaming or canceling white people. That should be clear to anyone who knows my work, especially if folks were to look at my season on *RHONY*. A lot of what I did on that show was rooted in an invitation for white people to get in greater relationship with their own humanity, and as part of that, to contemplate their own relationship to their whiteness, letting go of resentment, hesitancy, or hostility. In order to recognize and achieve the greatest level of humanity for themselves, it has to start there.

One of my absolute favorite activities is my mentoring work. And every second Monday of the month I hold Mentor Monday, mostly with young ladies. Some months ago, one of them wanted to ask me about *RHONY*. With some hesitation, she asked what much of the public also seemed to be wondering: How did I feel about being cast on *RHONY*? Hadn't they hired me because they, in the wake of George Floyd's murder, finally needed a Black Housewife?

In all fairness, even though this young lady was unin-formed about the timing of my being brought onto *RHONY*, as the casting process for a Black Housewife had begun before Floyd's murder, it was a good question, something that I would have asked if I was in a host seat. She deserved a clear answer, so I replied, "Let me tell you about the incred-ible power of the diversity hire." Or diversity *higher*, as we need to see it.

To all my beautiful *diversity highers* out there, know this: first, when you're hired because someone's hand has been forced, it always says so much more about them than you. That's the first important thing to remember. Whatever shame people try to project onto you isn't yours. I had affir-mative action shame thrown at my face as an undergrad at Chapel Hill all the time. Several white students perceived me as someone getting away with displacing the so-called rightful heir to a designated space of privilege. And I dealt with the same bullshit during my graduate school career, when I was a student at Loyola University's College of Law in New Orleans.

I'd transferred to Loyola from Southern University Law Center in Baton Rouge to finish my second year of law school. Loyola's campus was very traditional, with an old school look reminiscent of the popular 1973 legal dramedy *The Paper Chase*. The halls were peppered with plaques, framed documents, and photos that served as visual reminders of the institution's legacy. The student body consisted of individuals who were hyperambitious and hypercompetitive, there to prove a point about their academic prowess. The law program had a bit of a chip on its shoulder, and it was full of students with grit who wanted to show the world that they were as intelligent, competent, and formidable as their Harvard or Georgetown peers. The school has a particular reputation for producing exceptional trial attorneys with skills honed by their participation in national moot court competitions; as a result, these lawyers go on to prestigious, high-profile careers. I knew back then I wanted to be a trial attorney, or what we refer to as a talking lawyer, and I knew I wanted to be among the best, and so participating in the moot court was a no-brainer to me.

In order to enter the moot court trials, I'd have to participate in the Argue On competition. This is where students essentially "argue on" in front of a group of their peers in hopes of being chosen for one of Loyola's teams, with each team having a different focus. I had my heart set on being selected for the national team, the group that would get its name engraved on Loyola's massive marble wall of plaques that represented the school's preeminence in moot court work. They would go to the final competition in New York, the crown jewel of the contest. It was the most prestigious honor a student could have.

But my schoolmates scoffed, thinking it uncouth that as

a transfer student I had the audacity to participate in Argue On. And of course, this attitude was reinforced by my skin color. My majority white classmates made all sorts of comments about my academic potential, echoing sentiments I'd heard since elementary school: "You're not good enough..." "You don't really deserve it..." "You're going to hold us back..." "You're going to sully the reputation of our teams as winners..." "You're only here because of school quota requirements..." "You don't represent the best and brightest of us..." Essentially they wanted to know who I thought I was, as a Black woman and transfer student supposedly only on campus because of affirmative action initiatives, to attempt to occupy such rarified space like the moot court.

Those comments hurt, deeply. And then there was the pain I felt dealing with a few of my Black classmates who essentially expressed the same sentiments. For weeks I endured the drama mostly in silence. I understood that there were only so many slots available for each team on the moot court and students wanted to claim a space for themselves at all costs. But *shiiiit*, at the end of the day, I had every right to claim a space in the competition as well, regardless of the reasons I was on campus. So, after initially reeling from the criticisms, even questioning if my ambition was too much, I compartmentalized the emotional pain and adopted an inner and outer attitude of *fuck y'all!* toward my detractors. I got my ass together and diligently prepared for Argue

On, eventually making the national court team. I couldn't believe it. I was later told by the moot board that I'd presented the best argument they'd heard in years. The lessons of this moment would stay with me—that I need not place limitations on myself based on the judgment of others and that just because I benefited from race-based opportunities didn't make me any less qualified than my white peers.

During the national moot court competition, my team traveled to Oxford, Mississippi, to the University of Mississippi School of Law, aka Old Miss Law, to face off against the team from Louisiana State University's law center. Believe it or not, after several rounds of competition, the only two Black women participating—myself and another woman on the opposing team—made it to the final round. At the time I was a bit surprised, but nowadays I know this was by no means a coincidence. When you're Black and find yourself in these extremely white professional spaces, you're generally overqualified at whatever you've been called upon to do. (I don't know what happened to the sister in terms of her career, but wherever she is, I just bet she's fuckin' killing it!)

I won the competition for my team, basking in the glory of it all as I left that courtroom with the knowledge that I had proved the haters wrong, that regardless of what race-based or financial-hardship opportunities I had received, that I was a highly capable law student who could be a champion. And I share this because I want all of y'all to see yourselves in this way as well, to never allow anti-affirmative action rhetoric to get in the way of your self-assessment as someone who is qualified and capable of tremendous success. If you ever deal with the bullshit of anti-diversity hire rhetoric, whether you're a student on campus or at your workplace, your response needs to be this: "The fact that I'm here is because your instincts or the instincts of your forerunners were so malicious that you had to be forced into creating the bare-minimum opportunity for my ascension. This tells me everything I need to know about your lack of historical insight, and it says absolutely nothing about me."

Essentially, I want you to reallocate the fuckin' shame, which is really projected onto us just to make us feel small. Every aspect of American society has been calibrated to advantage the upper echelons of society. Systems have been put in place to make sure that we rarely ascend there. Here's what that means about our arrival and occupancy in rarified space: by the time we approach that threshold, we're already at least twice as good. Why? Because we've had to work twice as hard to have just as much as our white peers our entire fucking lives. When we finally arrive, with no previous professional networks or access to power via family and friends, with limited wealth to serve as a financial cushion, then we're going to kill it because we've been overpreparing. We're going to kill it because we're stepping into opportunity as a result of our education, hard work, intelligence, and talents.

Don't let them make you feel like you don't belong, *diversity higher*. You go right on into those rooms and be a disruptor. Blow the top off the lid and create some change, making a way for your people in that bitch.

We do ourselves a disservice and dishonor process when questioning our right to inhabit professional spaces, when feeling like we should be grateful to be allowed access to these spaces. I was inherently overqualified to be a Real Housewife of New York City. Look at what I had to bring to the table by way of being the first Black woman to be able to hold a coveted *Housewives* apple. I showed up with a plethora of social currencies and an oversupply of formal education not generally seen in the reality TV world. I had to have an advanced degree, a high-profile professional pedigree, and look good while being the show's youngest cast member. It was like I had to be Bravo TV's second coming of Vice President Kamala Harris to be seriously considered. Yet because I was essentially seen as a diversity hire, it was assumed that what I would contribute to the show would be subpar, that if it weren't for my skin color I would never have been allowed into such a supposedly rarified space.

Bitch, please. When you compare my experience to the bona fides held by my castmates, well, the double standard is clear. Half of them were college dropouts with mediocre academic credentials and, except for a couple, having no particular wealth-building mechanism that came from their own creation or design. They had access to wealth by virtue of who they married, and let's be clear, there's no shame in that. It just wasn't my choice, nor is it the path for millions of other Black people who make our way and generate income and social status by developing stellar skill sets. I see y'all, I hear y'all.

My understanding of how Black folks are generally overqualified for the positions we hold was reflected in my tagline for the show, which I'd actively campaigned for to use as my own. "I've had to work twice as hard for half as much, but now I'm coming for everything." To give you a bit of the behind-the-scenes scoop, the *RHONY* production company pushed back on that tagline several times. Their process is to let you create taglines of your own choosing, but they create taglines as well. And then we record about three or four options, with the executive powers that be ultimately picking the one they want to use in the show. Every time I would get an edit back on the taglines that they wanted me to record, the one that I wrote would be missing. By the time we went to the studio to record our taglines, I still made sure to record the line I'd come up with anyway. I eventually had to explain to the producers, "I know that you guys don't particularly like or understand this tagline. But I'm going to ask you to trust me here, that this is going to hit some textually the way it needs to. What I'm saying is very important, and you guys obviously have editorial control over all of this, but

I'm asking you to give me this one, to just trust me." And to their credit, despite the initial pushback, they did.

My tagline was obviously derived from the words that almost every Black person between the ages of nine and ninety has heard their whole life, which is that you have to work twice as hard for half as much. This is a reaction to an entrenched notion of anti-Blackness, according to which the larger white world will already think you're lazy, dumb, and dishonest. Just not up to par, not remotely good enough. And in order to succeed in life, it's not good enough to just be good enough. You've got to be twice as good. You've got to be overqualified and you need to overcompensate to contend with negative assumptions about who you are because of what you look like. As I approached *RHONY*, I wanted to address that head-on. And I also wanted to make it clear that my favorite part of the tagline was not the first part—it's not the "twice as hard for half as much" part—it's the "now I'm coming for everything" that I was excited about.

This part of the tagline referenced what I understood, when I was growing up, that you were expected to work twice as hard for half as much and then you take what you get. You take the leftovers, the crumbs or scraps, or whatever's available to you. But I wanted to turn this idea on its head. I hadn't done all this shit, and my ancestors hadn't done what they'd done to survive, for me to take some fuckin' crumbs. What folks had to know was that I'd worked my behind off, standing on the shoulders of those who'd come before me—and now I'm coming for everything and I'm not leaving until I get it.

I've gotta say it's my hope that more of us can adopt this attitude, especially when I look at the history of how Black people have been so blatantly sidelined and then given opportunities for which they're really more than qualified to handle. I've gotta go back to my girl Diahann Carroll one more time. I mean, I'm not going to complain that she earned a starring role on one of the top prime-time soaps of the era, but come on, y'all. That woman should have been given her own soap opera to star in as the lead with her own glamorous, fantastic Black family. (Chile, could you have imagined the ratings if a soap with *Dynasty* aesthetics and drama had been done for Black folks in the '80s? Would've been phenomenal.) I look at leaders in the corporate arena like Cynt Marshall, who worked for years at AT&T before becoming a corporate officer and then being brought on to be chief executive officer of the Dallas Mavericks, but only after the franchise had been marred by charges of rampant sexual harassment. Marshall strikes me as a patient soul whose spiritual faith is deeply inspiring, yet she speaks of how colleagues wouldn't fully understand her background and culture, and I believe this impacted how readily she was perceived to be a good fit for certain opportunities.

But the person who absolutely epitomizes being overqualified for her position is Washington, DC, native Ketanji Brown Jackson, who in early April 2022 was confirmed by the US Senate as the first Black woman Supreme Court justice. Even though she'd reached the highest court of the land through her impeccable credentials, she was nonetheless treated by some members of Congress as if she were underqualified for the role she'd be called upon to inhabit. Her ascension should have been cause for celebration for everyone, falling in line with her stellar professional history, like graduating cum laude from Harvard Law and working as vice chair of the US Sentencing Commission, which handled sentencing disparities and lowered the length of federal sentences. As a fellow former public defender and Black woman in the law, my heart was just beyond full when it came to Justice Jackson's Senate confirmation and subsequent swearing in in June. (I mean, can any of us forget the image of her daughter looking over at her mom with unadulterated pride during the confirmation hearings?)

But to my point about most Black people being overqualified for the positions they apply to or are considered for, here's this Black woman who did all the things that society says should qualify you for the crème de la crème of positions. She went to Harvard, arguably the best school in the nation—not once, but twice, for undergrad and law school—she clerked for the Supreme Court justice she was being nominated to replace, she worked at several standard

white-shoe law firms, and she was the first and only federal public defender to be nominated to sit on the Supreme
Court. Check, check, check, and then some. She'd done all
the things, and yet she was still being questioned by certain
pockets of this country and their political representatives
about her SAT scores and if she somehow enabled child pre-
dation because of her relatively thoughtful judicial rulings.
Give me a fucking break. What more proof do we need to
see that if you get caught up in this false narrative of seeking
"qualified status" as a Black American, you'll never get there.
It's important for us to create our own threshold of qualification, which isn't to be confused with mediocrity, as I don't
believe in that at all, but rather existing in a space where you
know you are operating at your self-assured best.

There's an element of Justice Jackson's career that really
must be singled out, which speaks to her overqualification
for being a Supreme Court justice—namely, that she worked
as a federal public defender. The law is the law. The American legal system is far from perfect, but to the extent it has a
shot in hell of having any level of success in terms of justice
being served, it requires the innate principle of adversary-
ness. This means you've got to have one side efficiently advocating against the other side, and then you have what we call
a tryer of fact. That's either a judge or jury making a legal
conclusion. That's our justice system in a nutshell. So when
it comes to criminal law, for instance, that means you've got

a prosecutor over here, trying to make a case on behalf of city, state, or government. And then you've got the defense, who's normally an individual or an entity arguing the exact opposite of the prosecution. That other side, that defense side, is routinely demonized. That defense side is often scrutinized and devalued, and what you have in our justice system is a kind of narrative in which the prosecutors— the assistant district attorneys, the district attorneys, the attorneys general—get to be the heroes. And thus a ton of our Supreme Court justices used to be prosecutors, fitting this heroic narrative. Very rarely does our society uphold and honor the extremely important and necessary work of defense lawyers. We see them as scum, as people defending guilty, awful people. And that's a bunch of bullshit, because if somebody didn't do the "dirty work" of defense lawyering, our system would fall on its face.

Justice Jackson has done the elite work of being a federal public defender. Anytime you talk about federal work, you're speaking of elite legal work, period. There're two tiers to our judicial system, state/local and federal. The federal tier has the most resources, and we expect more of it. So if you're a federal prosecutor, you've attained elite status. For Justice Jackson to be a federal public defender also means that she was working at an elite level. I was a public defender in Mecklenburg County in Charlotte, North Carolina, and I'm extremely proud of that work, but for her to be a public defender doing that work in a federal capacity speaks to her ability to see the complete purview of our justice system, and not have some of the bias that comes from individuals who've spent their entire legal career on only the prosecutorial side. Justice Jackson has seen all the sides of the justice system in a way that gives her a unique perspective and value in deliberating on cases. I believe this also speaks to her character and who she is.

At the end of the day, I'm overjoyed that Justice Jackson has been awarded a position that she so richly deserves, and more importantly, one that she seems happy to occupy. And I hope that all of y'all get to experience the opportunity of being awarded a position that accurately reflects your qualifications and tenacity and willingness to learn. But please remember, regardless of whether you've attained that sparkling moment of professional ascension via a diversity hire initiative, that you are qualified and have earned every right to be there, in that space, in that time, as someone who is beautiful, Black...qualified.

CHAPTER 9

SUMMATION

"It took many years vomiting up all the filth I'd been taught about myself, and half-believed, before I was able to walk on this earth as though I had a right to be here."

—JAMES BALDWIN

I N SUMMATION OF EVERYTHING I'VE STATED
previously about our journey in *Bet on Black*, I want
to invite my people, Black people, to vomit up all of
the filth, lies, offensive mythology, and dark tales that
have been associated with our humanity. Vomit up all of the
misconceptions and overt efforts to misassign the actuality
of Blackness. I invite the reader to purge all of the lies that
American culture has tried to force-feed us about who we
are, including that we're subordinate, that we're lazy, that
we're hypersexual (regardless of our gender identity), that
we're less than, that we're inherently second class or even
third class in the ways in which we occupy space.

I invite the reader to feel free to, as Baldwin proclaimed,

throw it up and throw it away. Because these notions of Blackness that came from outside of our community have always been a lie. They've always been a completely arbitrary, made up misassignment of what it is to be Black in this world and particularly what it means to be Black in America. Isabel Wilkerson in her book *Caste* does a beautiful job talking about the arbitrary nature of the American assignment of Blackness. And we know where it comes from. And I think this is very important. One could ask: "Why us? Why has the world, why has our homeland of America chosen to label us this way? Why have we been chosen to assign the most downtrodden, negative, lowly station of society and lived experience of Black people?" Some scholars have referred to the economic realities of the transatlantic slave trade, how Black humanity had to be disregarded in order to provide a justification for the mass enslavement of people that would fuel economies for centuries. Black subordination comes from complete dependence by whiteness—and not white people, mind you, but whiteness as a construct—on a system that operates in a zero-sum game that's rooted in notions of scarcity. This system says, "For me, a white person, to have, a Black person must have not. For a Black person to have, a white person must fall."

And we know this is untrue. Black people are a people of abundance; that is our culture, that is our history. And yet again, I invite y'all to look at the aggressive mislabeling of us as subordinate and as embodying all manner of horrific things—and then divorce yourself from it. As Baldwin once said, "I was not a 'nigger' even though you called me one. But if I was a 'nigger' in your eyes, there was something about you, there was something you [as a white person] needed." This was never our creation, these notions of Blackness. And thus we are entirely empowered to throw it up.

Now, as part of the good news in America today, we wholeheartedly know better. We intellectually know better, we academically know better. I'm not saying that we didn't know better yesterday and all the days before, but with history pushing us forward and the array of tools at our disposal, we absolutely know today for sure that we've been fed an avalanche of lies about our existence. And because we know it today for sure, we get to purge, vomit up the misinformation.

And when we purge, what do we put in its place? We cleanse our palate. We cleanse the space to tell a new story, an *accurate* story, going back to the first chapter of this book, about what Blackness actually is. We rid ourselves of the false notions of what it's not. And then we sit with the awesome work, the incredible, empowering work of actually defining Blackness for what it is. Blackness, from my lived experience, absolutely shines. It's beauty and ingenuity. It's tenacity and resilience, but not necessarily in ways steeped in trauma. It's a resilience on our own behalf, a resilience and tenacity that says we keep going because it's in our interest to keep going. And never for one second do we allow the outside world to question our innate intelligence, work ethic, or capabilities.

Blackness is a treasure, a superpower. It's the thing that courses through my bloodstream. It's the understanding of my own individual identity and where I fit into a broader collective identity as a people who are inherently connected to Africa. It's the African in us that makes us Black. And we don't need to run from, hide, or be ashamed of that. We get to relish our origins. Africa doesn't have to be perfect for our heritage to be powerful. And that's the thing, whether it's Black folks who are the descendants of those who were enslaved in America, whether it's Black folks still living on the continent, whether it's Black folks who're Ethiopian Jews in Israel, or Black folks in Germany, or Black folks in the UK, or Black folks in Jamaica or Haiti or the Dominican Republic or Puerto Rico...it doesn't matter. The thing that makes us all connected in the beauty of Blackness is the Africa in us. And I think that's incredibly powerful and really special. Also keep in mind that celebrating the Africa in all of us in no way undermines our inherent, intrinsic entitlement to American identity. The good news about being Black in America today is that one gets to marry identities if they choose. If you want to reject America for all of its atrocities, be my guest. I totally recognize that as a legitimate position. But it's also a legitimate position, one that I maintain for myself, to wholly maintain your entitled right to an American identity that harmoniously exists with your Blackness. We get to be as beautiful, proud, happy, joyful, and certain of ourselves as any other American.

In summation, I submit to the reader, if you've not done it already, throw up every nook and cranny of all the lies, all the nastiness, all the horrific things that America and the rest of the world have tried to force-feed you about what it means to be Black. Fill that space with the good news, the beautiful, layered, complicated story of Blackness. Fill that space with love, with light, with awesomeness, with that sweet special sauce. Some people call it magic, but I think Blackness is more intentional and has more certainty than that. Everything in this book is an invitation to allow yourself to embrace full liberation and the first-class citizenship that you're entitled to have. And part of that liberation is defining Blackness on your own terms, defining yourself for yourself.

I consider myself quite fortunate and very blessed that in my journey to getting in close relationship to my own Blackness I didn't have to do a whole lot of regurgitation— some, yes, but not a lot—because my dear mother, Gloria, did a pretty damned good job of ensuring that I had a pretty accurate picture from the beginning of what Blackness is. Among an array of other Black heroes, I understood the stories of Frederick Douglass and how he liberated his own self, so I never believed the myth of great white emancipators like Abraham Lincoln coming to our rescue. We as a people have always saved ourselves. We've certainly received aid from good-hearted, like-minded coconspirators outside the Black community, but we were at the heart of our liberation. We were always the engineers and masterminds of our freedom. That's not new and will probably never change. And really, why would we want it to?

You have every right to lead, to think critically, to offer solutions, to question deeply, to take up space and to occupy positioning at the highest level of any and every field you desire, at every mode of life you desire, to breathe, to con-template who you are and what works for you.

I submit to you that it is a treasure to be Black in America today. It is the place from which I draw my strength, my renewal, and my confidence, because the story I know of being Black is one of breathtaking competence. And that's why I walk into spaces and bring all of my Blackness with me, all the time, today. It's the place from which I know I'm most deserving to occupy space, to take up space, and to be my full and complete self. And that's what I invite you to do as well.

I want to particularly commend the great Black leaders of the civil rights era who negotiated on our collective behalf as Black folks occupying this land. Considering what the Black experience was like during that era, only a few generations removed from enslaved chattel existence…my God, what a remarkable job the leaders of that generation did to negotiate the terms of our existence. From the 1950s to the '70s, they created great statutory improvements with the goal of freeing us from blights such as redlining in the housing market, subpar educational access, workplace discrimination, and race-based terrorism. And to them I say, "Thank you, thank you, thank you." Sophisticated, remarkable, poignant negotiations were made on our behalf by those individuals.

And yet, more than fifty years have passed since we've last had those kinds of cohesive negotiations regarding what was permissible, what was expected, and what was available to us as Black people occupying space in our homeland here in America. Thus, the terms of those particular negotiations have expired. We could argue that they've *long* expired, and those terms, while a step in the right direction, were nowhere near the first-class existence that Black people in this country deserve.

If we wanted to pinpoint a particular expiration date for those terms, well, white folks declared it in 2020. White America fucked around and said, after the murder of George Floyd, "Ohmigod, we've treated Black people in this nation pretty horrifically! We sit in shock, awe, and horror as to how Black people are experiencing this nation and, ohmigod, we've gotta pause, stop, and reflect in the midst of this COVID pandemic and do something about it." That's what

RESOURCES

Eboni's Bet on Black Reading List

The 1619 Project: A New Origin Story by Nikole Hannah-Jones

African American Actresses: The Struggle for Visibility by Charlene B. Regester

All Boys Aren't Blue by George M. Johnson

All the Days Past, All the Days to Come by Mildred D. Taylor

The Autobiography of Malcom X by Malcom X and Alex Haley

The Bluest Eye by Toni Morrison

Brothers and Sisters by Bebe Moore Campbell

Caste: The Origins of Our Discontents by Isabel Wilkerson

The Fire Next Time by James Baldwin

Hidden Figures: The American Dream and the Untold Story of the Black Women Mathematicians Who Helped Win the Space Race by Margot Lee Shetterly

How to Succeed in Business Without Being White: Straight Talk on Making It in America by Earl G. Graves

RESOURCES

I Know Why the Caged Bird Sings by Maya Angelou

Logan Family Saga Series by Mildred D. Taylor

A Mercy by Toni Morrison

Narrative on the Life of Frederick Douglass, an American Slave by Frederick Douglass

Notes of a Native Son by James Baldwin

Phillis Wheatley: Complete Writings by Phillis Wheatley

The Souls of Black Folk by W.E.B. Du Bois

A Testament of Hope: The Essential Writings and Speeches by Martin Luther King Jr., edited by James M. Washington

Your Blues Ain't Like Mine by Bebe Moore Campbell

ABOUT THE AUTHOR

EBONI K. WILLIAMS is the host and executive producer of the Warner Music Group podcast *Holding Court with
Eboni K. Williams*. In addition to starring on *The Real Housewives of New York* and guest hosting *The View*, she is currently the host of *The Grio with Eboni K. Williams*, which
airs on a cable television network owned by Byron Allen.
She also hosts a true crime series that is featured on the
OWN and Investigation Discovery networks. Williams is an
attorney and a frequent public speaker on Black culture and
history. Williams lives and owns in Harlem, USA.